Dreamkeepers

ALSO BY HARVEY ARDEN

Wisdomkeepers

WITH STEVE WALL

Dreamkeepers

A Spirit-Journey into
Aboriginal Australia

HARVEY ARDEN

Photographs by Harvey Arden and Mike Osborn

HarperCollins*Publishers*

HarperCollins books may be purchased
for educational, business, or sales
promotional use. For information please
write: Special Markets Department,
HarperCollins Publishers, Inc., 10 East
53rd Street, New York, NY 10022.

FIRST EDITION
Jacket and interior design
by Aufuldish & Warinner

Library of Congress Cataloging-in-
Publication Data

Arden, Harvey.
    Dreamkeepers : a spirit-journey into
aboriginal Australia / Harvey Arden ;
photographs by Harvey Arden and Mike
Osborn. — 1st ed.
    p.   15.5 x 23.5 cm.
    ISBN 0-06-016916-8 (cloth)
    1. Australian aborigines—Australia—
Kimberley (W.A.)—Social life and
customs. 2. Mythology, Australian
aboriginal—Australia—Kimberley (W.A.)
3. Philosophy, Australian aboriginal—
Australia—Kimberley (W.A.) I. Title.
GN667.W5A73   1994
299'.92—dc20   93-21284

94 95 96 97 98 ❖/CW 10 9 8 7 6 5 4 3 2 1

*This book is dedicated to
the Aboriginal peoples of Australia,
to Aboriginal peoples everywhere,
and to the Aboriginal in each of us.*

Hear, you mob!
I'm an Aboriginal.
I'm an Australian.
I'm a Miriwoong.
We're all one family,
All together,
We human beings.
All one big mob!
—Ted Carlton, Miriwoong

Contents

· · ▲ · ·

Color-photograph section follows page 112.

Author's Note

Only infrequently during my travels in the Kimberley did I hear people use the word *Aborigine,* which has a vaguely clinical ring to it despite being perfectly proper. Almost always the expression was *Aboriginal people* or just *Aboriginals,* and I have adopted this usage here.

The word *Aboriginal,* used as both noun and adjective, derives from the Latin:

> *Ab* "from" or "out of"
> *origin* "beginning" or "source"
> *al* "one belonging to"

Interestingly, the Latin *origo* also means "I rise" or "I become visible." Hence, an "Aboriginal" might be defined as "One from the Beginning who is rising and becoming visible."

The author wishes to thank the staff of the Australian Embassy in Washington, D.C., especially Counsellor for Public Affairs Christopher Sweeney, for the use of their research facilities, for transportation assistance via Qantas Airways as part of the Visit Australia Program, and—not least—for their warm encouragement over the years.

Grateful acknowledgment is made for permission to reprint the following copyright material:

The title poem by Daisy Utemorrah from *Do Not Go Around the Edges*, 1990, Magabala Books Aboriginal Corporation, Broome, Western Australia.

Lyrics from the song "Treaty" in the album *Tribal Voice* by the musical group Yothu Yindi, 1992, Australian Mushroom Music (ASCAP).

Dreamkeepers

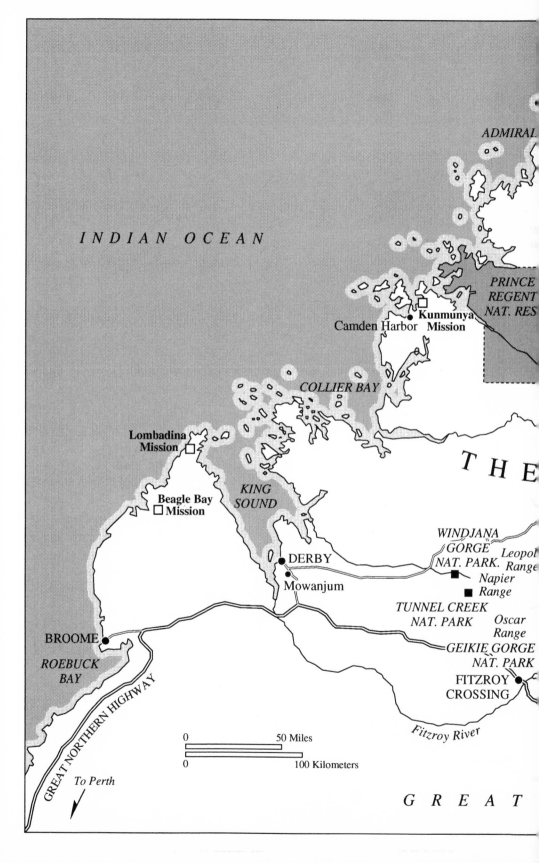

ADMIRAL

INDIAN OCEAN

*PRINCE
REGENT
NAT. RES*

□ Kunmunya
Camden Harbor **Mission**

COLLIER BAY

Lombadina
Mission □

*KING
SOUND*

Beagle Bay
□ **Mission**

T H E

● DERBY
● Mowanjum

*WINDJANA
GORGE* *Leopol
Range*
NAT. PARK.
■ *Napier
Range* ■

*TUNNEL CREEK
NAT. PARK* *Oscar
Range*

BROOME ●

*ROEBUCK
BAY*

GEIKIE GORGE
NAT. PARK

FITZROY ●
CROSSING

Fitzroy River

GREAT NORTHERN HIGHWAY

0   50 Miles

0   100 Kilometers

To Perth

G R E A T

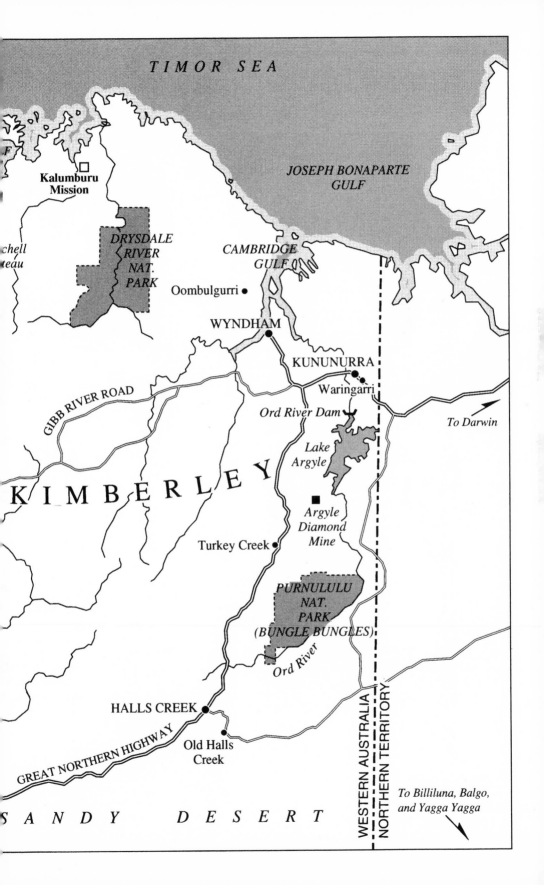

WARNING
YOU ARE NOW ENTERING AN ABORIGINAL RESERVE

Entry to this reserve is restricted to Aboriginals, Authorised persons and Permit holders only.
It is mandatory that a permit be obtained before travelling through Aboriginal Reserves.

For enquiries

Aboriginal Affairs Planning
Authority (AAPA)
P.O.Box 628
West Perth   **AND**
Western Australia 6005.
or Phone (09) 322 7044

Penalties for breach

In accordance with section 31 of the Aboriginal Affairs Planning Authority Act it is an offence to enter an Aboriginal Reserve without permission.

The act provides for a fine/or term of imprisonment or both for breach of condition.   BY ORDER
COMMISSIONER FOR ABORIGINAL PLANNING

Get Your Own Dreamtime

• • • • •

"YOU'LL NEVER DISCOVER the blackfella's secret," said the Aboriginal man in the flowered Hawaiian shirt, sitting on the concrete veranda of his small house just outside the remote port town of Wyndham, Western Australia, drinking a can of Diet Coke and confronting the two unannounced visitors before him with distrusting eyes.

He was in his midthirties, a burly man, clean-cut, light skinned for an Aboriginal. My Aussie guide, Mike Osborn, who'd lived here in Australia's far northwest for more than twenty years, had recommended him to me as an interesting "young bloke," extremely intelligent and well spoken, a respected local community leader with strong opinions on matters Aboriginal. Someone, in short, "well worth havin' a yarn with," as Mike put it.

He'd welcomed the two of us with a noncommittal nod, gesturing for us to sit down across from him at the small veranda table. Planting his elbows on the edge of the table and resting his chin on the knuckles of his clasped hands, he eyed us with knowing suspicion.

He continued: "So don't you whitefellas come round here snif-fin' after our Dreamtime stories like all those others do, those anthros and those journos and all them. Sure, maybe you get me to tell you a story from our Dreamtime, then you take it and write it down in your book and sell it for a million dollars. You white blokes are all the same. Can't you understand? It's not mine to give you, that story. I don't own it. It's the property of my people. . . .

"It's like . . . it's like a watch, a gold watch. Like I'm wearing the gold watch my father gave me and you ask me the time. So I tell you the time. But I don't give you the watch, too, do I? Whitefella now, he asks for the time and then he wants to take the watch, too! That's the Gadia way, the whitefella way. So don't you come here askin' me for any of our Dreamtime stories. Get your own Dreamtime. Don't take ours."

THE WORDS STUNG. I confess, I *had* hoped to garner a few stories from the Dreamtime on this "spirit-journey" of mine into Aborig-inal Australia. For more than a dozen years I had traveled among the Indian peoples of North America, seeking out their traditional spiritual elders and recording their words for a book I eventually coauthored with writer-photographer Steve Wall — *Wisdomkeepers: Meetings with Native American Spiritual Elders* (Beyond Words Publishers, 1990).

As part of my personal compact with those Native American elders, I had agreed at the outset to steer clear of so-called secrets and to avoid asking questions about sacred rituals and cere-monies not meant for outsiders' eyes, ears, or presence. Such matters were patently none of my business, and any probings in that direction, I was warned repeatedly, would bring me not only certain rejection but possible spiritual, even physical harm.

Instead, I made it my practice to ask them no prearranged questions, but to let our conversations roam and take us wherever they might. Quite beyond my expectations, the elders were soon sharing with me their innermost thoughts and emotions, their poignant personal memories, their visions, their healing remedies, their creation stories and apocalyptic prophecies. It was my job simply to listen to them and keep out of the way as best I could, faithfully and reverently taking down their words.

I was no anthropologist or scholar or historian. I wasn't *study-ing* them. Indigenous people aren't specimens to be studied. They're not curiosities to be gawked at. They aren't "quaint." They're not "primitive." They aren't some kind of "childlike" version of ourselves, whomever we may mean by "ourselves." They're here *now*, as much a part of this "modern" world as anyone else on the planet. I wanted to relate to them as human being to human being, no more . . . but *no less*.

ALL OF THIS, it had seemed to me, could be applied equally well to the Aboriginal people of Australia, custodians of the oldest culture on earth, keepers of the Dreamtime. I call them Dream-keepers.

I'd been tremendously impressed by my brief but memorable encounters with them while writing a magazine article on north-west Australia the year before and had found my hard-bitten journalist's soul smitten by their spiritual notion of the Dream-time, also known as the Dreaming or simply the Dream. Perhaps nothing in Aboriginal culture has such allure for the Western mind—the Gadia or whitefella mind, as this man would call it. It is a concept both highly charged and wonderfully elusive. To define it is to define the indefinable.

On the one hand, in Aboriginal belief, the Dreamtime was a Genesis-like epoch in which ancestral creator figures—chief among them the Rainbow Snake, the Lightning Brothers, and, in some areas of the far northwest, the Wandjina, or Cloud-Beings—traveled on epic adventures across earth's originally featureless topography, giving shape in the course of colossal struggles and battles to each mountain and river and gorge, each jutting rock and billabong, or water hole. In the process they populated the primordial landscape with the founding ancestors—part human, part animal, part divine—of today's Aboriginal peoples.

On the other hand, in a seeming paradox—at least to outsiders—the Dreamtime isn't a past epoch at all. Rather, it exists as a kind of metaphysical *now*, a mystical time outside of time, a spiritual yet nonetheless *real* dimension of time and space somehow interpenetrating and concurrent with our own. To Aboriginals, it lies just around the corner of the mind and perceptions, and, in a sense, can be physically entered by initiates—and only by initiates—during ceremonies and dreams. There, in that otherworldly realm, the Ancestor Beings still exist as always, continually renewing and maintaining the land and the cycle of seasons—indeed, the whole Universe—through a mystical communion with their loving Aboriginal descendants.

To this day Aboriginal groups and individuals trace their particular ancestry, or Dreaming, to one or more of these Dreamtime demigods. When an Aboriginal says, "I have a Crocodile Dreaming" or "I'm a Dingo Dreaming man," he refers to the Dreamtime Crocodile or the ancestral creator Dingo, who helped shape the landscape in that long-ago time and to whom he bears a special affinity and spiritual relationship.

An Aboriginal with a Crocodile or a Dingo Dreaming, for instance, would never kill or eat a crocodile or dingo; to him or her that would be a virtually cannibalistic desecration. Rather, the very existence and increase of that particular Dreaming species depends, in Aboriginal belief, on the strict performance of the appropriate seasonal rituals—dances, song-and-story cycles, and so on—that bring them into direct metaphysical contact with the Ancestor Beings.

When Aboriginals go Walkabout—their version of the American Indian's vision-quest or spirit-journey—they aren't wandering randomly through the bush but are rigorously following preordained routes through their family's own particular inherited portion of Dreaming country along the Tracks of the Ancestors. As they go, these days more often by car or truck than on foot, they stop at each ancestral sacred site to perform the prescribed ancient ceremonies, or *corroborees*—secret-sacred versions of the open and nonsacred corroborees so popular among tourists to Aboriginal Australia.

Stories recounting the epic Dreamtime adventures of the Ancestor Beings are told not as bedtime stories for children but as mnemonic devices to teach the listeners an absolutely essential working knowledge of their own immediate physical environment, how to travel safely through it and how to relate to the other living creatures and plants with whom they share it and to whom they bear a special responsibility and familial kinship. Like Aboriginal songs, paintings, and ceremonies, these Dreamtime stories are not mere entertainments but a combination of history, moral homily, and practical how-to instruction in geographical orienteering, etching the lay of the vast local landscape into each individual's memory. To an outsider they may seem charming or quaint, vaguely reminiscent of Greco-Roman myths or Aesop's *Fables*, but to Aboriginals they are at once sacred parables and indispensable road maps through the terrain of their home territory.

Of such matters I had read but knew nothing firsthand.

MOVED BY THE sheer poetry and spiritual power of these Aboriginal concepts, I had decided—presumptuously, no doubt—to make this spirit-journey of mine back to northwest Australia's remote and spectacular Kimberley region to meet and mingle souls, if you will, with the extraordinary people who had created them. Say that I was looking for a Dreaming of my own—an absurdity for an outsider, perhaps, but, to me, a lovely absurdity, resonant with meanings.

And, of course—crass Gadia motive—I would write a book about the experience. No longer a journalist, having dropped out of that arcane profession after practicing it for more than a quarter of a century with infinite devotion and arrogance, I was at best a down-at-heels private author these days —"the Awtha," as my guide Mike pronounced it with amused scorn to all we met— and at worst an over-the-hill cultural voyeur here to warm my hands over the fading embers of another people's dying culture.

And now, this Aboriginal man in the flowered Hawaiian shirt—the first "subject" of my Australian journey—was proving decidedly uncooperative, even hostile. On our arrival, grudgingly agreeing to speak to us at all, he had immediately waved off our tape recorder and cameras.

"Don't need those," he said. "Just listen and remember what I say."

Not exactly an auspicious beginning for the Awtha.

"You mind if I take notes?" I asked.

The Aboriginal shrugged, fairly glaring at me.

After all, I was Gadia. White man. Whitefella. We, Mike and I—in the local Kriol or Pidgin dialect—were *dugadia*. Two white men. Coupla whitefella. Bad Blokes. Watch 'm.

His eyes were like blows. I could hardly avoid flinching.

To ease into our conversation, I'd asked him if he knew any Dreamtime stories about the origins of the boab—the wondrous bottle tree, or baobab, which, in Australia, grows almost exclusively in this wild Kimberley region. It had seemed an innocent enough question.

But this angry young Aboriginal was on to me. *"Get your own Dreamtime. Don't take ours."*

I was shaken. He was right. I'd come for something . . . something that wasn't mine. And, it was true, I'd planned to take it away, show it to others . . . even sell it to them in the form of a book. Righto, mate. Make a buck, you know.

And he wasn't buying it, this Aboriginal. He wasn't taking my hook. I was left with an empty line dangling over the immense void between us. I had wanted to bridge that void and now found myself about to fall right into it.

I figured the conversation was at an end. But then, having dismissed my line of questioning, the Aboriginal man took the situation in hand.

"Let's talk about Aboriginal dignity, not Dreamtime stories," he said. "That's what you *should* be writin' about in your bloody book."

He was finally talking after all. I started jabbing away in my notebook, rapidly scribbling the phrases as he spoke. I have reconstructed his words here as best I can.

THE VIOLENCE INSIDE US

"Aboriginal dignity is coming back," he said, "but it's coming back in a violent way."

"How is it violent?" I asked.

"It's violent because it has to overcome violence."

"You mean . . . revolution?" I asked. "Armed revolt?"

He shook his head, scorn tightening his lips.

"We Aboriginals make up barely one percent of the people in Australia, mate. You think we're going to pick up guns and start a revolution to overthrow the government? No, it's not violence against white people I'm talking about. It's the violence inside us, the violence Gadia planted inside us and left growin' there. . . .

"When I was a boy back in the fifties, the coppers around Wyndham here used to shoot blackfellas for ten bob a head. So that's where we got the violence. Things like that, a million things like that. And now it's all coming out, it's spilling out of us, but it's a violence directed against ourselves, not against whites.

That's the sad thing. Mostly it's violence against ourselves.

"Our young people get pissed on the grog and get in fights and kill each other. They go to jail and hang 'mselves in their cells. No one knows why, 'cause that's not the Aboriginal way, to kill yourself. We never committed suicide in the old days. We never believed in that. 'Deaths in custody' the government calls it. They even made a bloody commission to study it!"

"So where does the dignity come in?" I asked. The notions of Aboriginal dignity, on the one hand, and Aboriginal violence against themselves, on the other, didn't quite seem to jibe in my mind as they did in his.

His broad nostrils flared. His eyes burned into me. I was infuriating him. He bit off his words as he spoke.

"The dignity comes from overcoming the violence, mate. Don't you see? It comes from not letting the violence destroy us from the inside. We're not all that way, you know. We don't all get pissed on the grog and fight and kill each other. Me, I could be that way, too, but I'm not. I chose not to. I had some school, I got a job, I pay taxes. . . . I don't want their bloody pension check every other Tuesday, their 'sit-down money' like they call it, so we can go out and sit on the ground under a boab tree and drink ourselves into oblivion. That's not for me. Dignity is overcoming that, overcoming the violence inside us, the violence that *you*, the Gadia, put there.

"So now the Gadia are feeling guilty," he went on. "They decided to give us back some land, some of our own lost land that they stole years ago and pushed us off of. . . . Well, now *that* I'll bloody well take! My mob, my family here in Wyndham, we got a little block of land they're givin' us back. See that range of hills out there, across the Gulf and on the other side? We own a piece of that, our mob does. They said we could have that back, that little part of what we once had. So we're gettin' ready to go back to the country, back out bush, gonna build ourselves a place to live out there. An 'outstation' they call it. We know they're just doing it to get rid of us, get us out of the way, but we don't care. We *like* bein' out of the way, off by ourselves, away from all the humbug here in town. We're not going to cry about what happened in the past. We're looking toward the future, not the bloody past. That's what I mean by dignity."

BLACKFELLA'S LAW

"And so," I asked, "out there in the bush you'll go back to the old ways and get away from the violence?"

Again he shook his head at my question, taking a deep sip of Diet Coke and setting the can down hard on the table.

"The old ways aren't for me, mate. Not anymore. I was born in the bush. I remember how it used to be with the old people back then. But those days are gone. Gone for good. We can't go back. We're caught, Aboriginal people like me, caught between the old ways and Gadia's way. We don't want either one. 'Course, you'll find plenty who'll disagree with me, traditional blackfellas who think we *should* go back. . . .

"Gadia thought they killed the old Law, but it's gettin' strong again, it's comin' back strong. They come here, those Law Men—Aboriginal Law Men, I mean, not your Gadia coppers. They come out of the desert in the middle of the night, those Law Men, come with their Toyotas and their rifles and they take the youngfellas, grab 'm right outa their homes and take 'm out bush for ceremony, to initiate 'm into the old Law. They cut 'm, you know—what you call circumcise 'm. 'Make 'm men, those boys,' that's what the Law Men say. Just like the old days. But we don't do that around here anymore. We gave it up. We don't like it. If the boys make trouble, if they're bad, the Law Men beat 'm up, beat the crap out of 'm. Sometime, if those youngfellas keep doin' it, keep bein' bad, doin' more humbug, the Law Men'll spear 'm in the thigh or hit 'm in the head with a *nulla*

nulla, a war club. Sometime those Law Men even kill 'm.

"Me, now, I want no bloody part o' that. I don't want that old Law anymore. The Gadia killed it and it's gone. So let it die, that's what I say. Let its ghost go someplace else and stop botherin' us, that old Law. I'm an Aboriginal man and I'm bloody proud of it, but that doesn't mean I want the old Law. I don't want anybody takin' *my* boys and cuttin' 'm. Livin' under that blackfella Law is worse than livin' under Russian communism. It's violent, a violent Law. Just like the Gadia law. They're different but they're the same. Violent. Both of 'm, violent Laws."

WHITEFELLA'S RELIGION

And now the conversation took an even more surprising turn. He leaned forward across the table, locking his intense brown eyes on mine.

"But white man's *religion,* now . . . me, I say that it's better'n blackfella's. Blackfella's religion's no bloody good. Whitefella's God is better'n blackfella's, don't you think?"

I shrugged, wrenching my eyes away from his, more than a bit nonplussed. It seemed a curious question. Here I'd traveled halfway around the planet to get at the meaning, the essence of Aboriginal spiritual belief—that part of it, at least, that was accessible to an outsider—and this fellow was telling me that it was "no bloody good."

"I'll tell you why I think so," he went on. "I was Catholic for thirty years and that's about the only thing I liked about it—the whitefella's God, this Jesus fella, all this Father and Son and Holy Ghost and all that. . . . I liked that. Better'n blackfella's God, better'n Rainbow Snake and all that. That's all gone now. Whitefella's God won out over blackfella's Snake. So Gadia's God is better'n blackfella's, eh? There are some who'll tell you different, but that's what I think anyway. . . .

"So that's why I say you better stop lookin' for the blackfella's secret and stick with your own whitefella's God. That's why I say you'll never discover the blackfella's secret. And even if you did, you'd only be sorry. It's not your secret, and it could hurt you, could even kill you. Same with the Dreamtime stories. They're not your stories. They're not for children like your fairy tales. Don't write your book about those like all those anthros and journos do, comin' here and stealin' our stories.

"Write about the real blackfella, the blackfella today. . . . Write about how he's gettin' back his dignity."

HE LEANED BACK in his chair and took an emphatic swig of the Diet Coke. His chest was heaving with emotion. He seemed drained. Perhaps he'd said more than he'd intended. An exchange of glances made it clear it was time to go. Mike and I stood up, shook his hand, and started to leave. The Aboriginal man had one final comment as he walked us to the car.

"And I prefer you don't use my name, either," he said. "That's mine, too, and I'm not givin' it out to just anyone. Look at your notes on what I said, write 'm up, then send me your bloody book when it comes out and I'll read it.

"I wanna see how you lie about what I say."

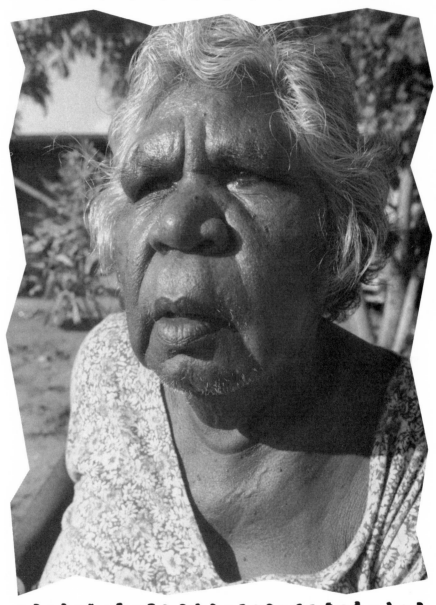

DAISY UTEMORRAH—THE STORYTELLER OF MOWANJUM:

"Words are my gun and my spear."

1

The Storyteller of Mowanjum

THEY WERE WAITING at Mowanjum. Storyteller Daisy Utemorrah was waiting. Her husband, Lorrie, was waiting. All of Mowanjum was waiting.

They had been waiting for years. . . .

"THEY CALLED US last week and told us to come on up to Mitchell Plateau to talk to 'm about finally givin' back the land," said Lorrie. "They said they'd have a car come and pick us up here at Mowanjum. Said they'd drive us out to the airport and take us on up to Mitchell Plateau in an airplane. Supposed to be here yesterday, but they never came."

"*Who* told you?" Mike asked.

"Government blokes. Blokes from the mining company."

"Which? Government blokes or mining blokes?"

Lorrie shrugged. "I dunno. Gadia blokes. You know? Said the papers were all ready to sign. Said we could sign 'm and then we could go back, leave Mowanjum and go live back where we come from. That's my country up there on Mitchell Plateau, my people's country. Wunambal country. Years ago they made us get out, said they had to do their minin' up there. Bauxite. That's aluminum, you know. Whole Mitchell Plateau is made outa the bloody stuff! Told us when they were through minin' we could go back and live there again. They been promisin' us I don't know how long. . . . How long is it now, Daisy?"

"Fourteen year I think," said his wife, sitting by herself on a thin-mattressed cot a few feet away.

"Yup, fourteen year we been waitin'. Mebbe longer. Seems longer. So we were glad when they called us last week. Wanted us to come up right then, they said. I told 'm Daisy was in the hospital. She had a stroke a few weeks back, you know. She couldn't come right then, I told 'm. Come by and get us on Sunday after she gets back, I said. We'll be waitin' for you. So we packed our bags and waited."

He waved a hand toward two strapped plastic suitcases behind Daisy's cot on the concrete-slab veranda.

"But the car never came to pick us up. We sat out here waitin' all day. Never came to get us. No car. No plane. We got no way of gettin' up there to Mitchell Plateau, you know. No way at all. Daisy and me, we both had strokes. So how we gonna get up there? How we gonna sign the papers to get back the land?"

"Can't you call them back to see what the problem is?" I asked.

"Don't know who to call," said Lorrie. "Some government blokes, I called 'm from the phone over at the Mowanjum office. Said they'd try and find out for me what's goin' on. But they never called us back."

"That's what happened before," Daisy interjected. "Happened lots of times. They promise but nothin' ever happens."

"Maybe they'll come today," Lorrie said hopefully. "We thought maybe you was them comin' up in your Toyota there. Oh, well. We been waitin' so long I guess we can wait a while longer."

•　•　•　•　•

As MIKE AND I had driven through the gate at Mowanjum, we'd passed an old battered sign that had fallen off the fence post and now lay rotting in the brush, its lettering cracked and peeling:

1788–1988

Bicentennial of Our Sorrow

We'd come here to the Mowanjum Aboriginal Reserve, on the edge of Derby in the west Kimberley, to see Daisy Utemorrah, noted Aboriginal poet and storyteller, author of several books, including one I'd bought in Broome, *Do Not Go Around the Edges* (Magabala Books, Broome, W.A., 1990).

"You can talk to her Awtha to Awtha," Mike commented wryly. "Besides, she's a great lady, old Daisy is. None finer. Same for Lorrie, her husband. He's one of the bossmen here at Mowanjum. Fine a bloke as you'll find."

We drove through the red-dirt bleakness that is Mowanjum, heading for some low government-built houses. Garbage lay strewn everywhere, assiduously tended by the usual scruffy camp dogs, who lurked about like accusations. At first glimpse the place looked abandoned. It was hard for me to believe people actually lived here.

"Gotta see past it, mate," Mike said. "Try to see it through their eyes, which means not seein' it at all. . . . They just don't see all that trash and crap lyin' around. . . . They see right through it. In the old days, when camp got dirty, why, they'd just pick up their stuff and go. . . . Well, they're *still* plannin' to pick up and go, even after all these years. So why pick up the garbage? No way you're ever goin' to change 'm, not the older folks anyway. They're still livin' on the edges of the Dreamtime, waitin' to go back in."

The edges of the Dreamtime . . . that's where I'd come to, I realized. My original idea had been to make a journey *into* the Dreamtime, but already I was beginning to see that that would be quite impossible. Even getting to the *edges* of the Dreamtime was problematical.

Should I even be *there?*

The title poem of Daisy's *Do Not Go Around the Edges* suggested the edges themselves were dangerous:

> *Do not go around the edges*
> *or else you'll fall.*
> *No good that place*
> *or else you slip.*

I took a personal meaning in those words. Even at the edges I'd have to watch my step, keeping to the safe ground.

I recall the words of an American Indian elder who'd told me: "Everyone got to find the right path. You can't see it so it's hard to find. No one can show you. Each person's got to find the path by himself."

Another Indian elder had added: "It's the path to the Creator. That's the only path there is."

So here I was, trying to follow that invisible path—and it had led me halfway around the world to Mowanjum. As an outsider, as Gadia, I would have to tread cautiously. Even if I couldn't go into that Aboriginal Dreamtime, I could reverently and respectfully skirt the edges as best I was able, getting lightninglike glimpses here and there. At times I would see the light from the Dreamtime the way you see light coming out from under the closed door of a brilliantly illuminated room. And yet, to me, the door was forever locked. I'd have to learn to live with that.

"There's Daisy's house," Mike said, heading toward one of the houses where half a dozen Aboriginal people were gathered, sitting abjectly on a concrete veranda. They somehow had the look of refugees waiting to be rescued.

Having already been properly chastised about "stealin' our Dreamtime stories" by the angry young Aboriginal man in Wyndham, I was now suspicious of my motives for being here.

After all, Daisy Utemorrah was probably the best-known teller of Dreamtime stories in the Kimberley. If I couldn't talk to her about those, what would we talk about?

Would she speak to us at all?

BUT THEY COULDN'T have been more friendly and welcoming. While we spoke with Lorrie and several other of the men about the problems up at Mitchell Plateau, Daisy sat on the cot on the veranda a few feet away and thumbed through a copy of my book *Wisdomkeepers*. Mike had explained to her that we hoped she would agree to be part of a similar book on Aboriginal people, and she had nodded pleasantly enough but without commitment. I could hear her murmuring "Mmmm . . . Mmmm" as she slowly turned the pages.

"You . . . ," she said after several minutes.

"Me?" asked Mike.

"No, *you*," Daisy said, looking at me.

"Oh"—Mike smiled—"You mean the Awtha here."

"Mmmm. You, come here, sit on down beside me. We'll talk for a while."

I walked over and sat beside her on the edge of the veranda.

"You know all these Indian people in this book here?" she asked.

"I do."

"Mmmm. I like what they say. Good words. True words. You say you want to put my words in a book like this?"

"Yes, if you'd like to. That's why I've come."

"Good people, those Indian people," she said. "Good people like Aboriginal people. We think the same, just like the Indian. You know this fella here, this . . . what's his name . . . Mathew King?"

She'd opened the book to the pages on Lakota spiritual elder Mathew King.

"Good fella him, this Mathew King. He talk just like black-fella. You see here . . . him talkin' about the Black Hills? How he wants 'm back for his people, those sacred hills? Just like our country, our sacred Mitchell Plateau. Look here . . . what's this he's sayin'?"

Her fingernail underscored the words.

"'The Black Hills aren't for sale.' See? Just like us. Indian's just like blackfella. Same thing. They want their land back. Only the land. They don't want money, they don't want millions and millions of dollars. They just want the land back. That's what we want, too. Not money. Just the land. The land, the ground, the sand, you know? That's all we want. Just to go back and live there, to sit down on the ground and *be* there, doin' whatever we like, listen to the wind, listen to the rain, listen to the stars. Just like the Indian. Just like your Mathew King here. You still see him, this Mathew King? I'd like to meet him and talk with him."

"I'm sorry to say he's passed on now," I said.

"Mmmm. Too bad. But mebbe he's back with the land now, you know? Maybe he's happy now."

"I hope so. He was a wonderful man."

"So now you want my words, too? Is that it? Dreamtime stories . . . is that what you come here to get?"

"If you like," I said. "Anything you'd like to talk about, Daisy. Some people have told me it's not right for Gadia to write down your stories. They say you shouldn't write them down unless they're your own stories."

"True. It's true. I tell Dreamtime stories all the time, you know. Tell 'm all over the country. I know lots of Dreamtime stories. Lots of 'm. People like to hear 'm. I write 'm down in my books. But they're not mine, those stories. They belong to my people, the Worrora people. Lorrie, he's Wunambal. He'll tell you Wunambal stories. I tell you Worrora stories. Different people, different stories. Belong only to the people they belong to. They got . . . what you call it . . . a *copyright*. Them stories, they're copyright by their own people. Worrora by Worrora. Wunambal by Wunambal. Nobody else. Not by you, not by anyone but their own people.

"Just like the land, you know. The land, it's copyright too. . . . We black people got the copyright but Gadia, he went and stole it."

SHE NODDED AT my tape recorder.

"You gonna turn that on, that tape thing? You gonna take my words?"

"Only with your permission, Daisy."

"But no Dreamtime stories," she said. "You want those, you go buy my books. *Visions of Mowanjum*, that's one. *Dhunby the Turtle*, that's one, too. I see you got *Do Not Go Around the Edges* there. That's my new one. You want me to sign it for you?"

"I'd love that," I said.

"And here, you sign me your book, too."

We exchanged signatures. Awtha to Awtha. Copyright to copyright.

"Good," Daisy said. "Now turn it on, that tape thing, and hold it up close to me here. I can't talk too loud since I had my stroke."

I pressed the record button.

LISTEN TO MY WORDS

"Here's my words. You listen. I want people to hear them. Long long time ago, in the early-early days, our black people fought the white people with spears, they fought 'm with guns, you know? But these days we only fight with words. Fighting with spears and guns is no good for us black people anymore. It doesn't work. Our people fought with spears and guns and still they lost the land. So that's why I'm a storyteller. That's why I'm a writer. I fight with words. I fight with words for my people. I'm gonna take the land back with words. Words are my gun and my spear.

"The government, they use words, too. They plenty good at using words just like they used to be plenty good at using guns. They stopped using guns on us black people now. Now they use words on us. They come here to Mowanjum, they have a talk-talk-talk with us. Lotsa times they come. Lotsa talk-talk-talk. Plenty meetings, meetings, meetings. They tell us they gonna do

DAISY AND LORRIE

this and they gonna do that. They tell us they gonna give Mitchell Plateau back to us so we can go and live there.

"They tell us when they're through diggin' holes for all the aluminum we can have the land back. Oh, no, not all the land, just a little piece of the land. Just the size of a matchbox."

She drew a large rectangle in the red dirt with the tip of her cane—an aluminum cane, as if in some kind of perverse symbolism. Inside the larger rectangle she drew a tiny rectangle.

"There! That's it! Just a matchbox! Nothing but a little matchbox! They want us to go and live in a matchbox! Now, here, you look at this—" She redrew the larger outer rectangle.

"You see? That's what we had before they came, that's what they took from us so they could dig their holes. That's Lorrie's land, his people's land. Wunambal land. My own people's land, Worrora land, that's way over there. They took that, too. The old people who lived there are gone from there now. They don't live there anymore. And that—" She redrew the tiny inner rectangle. "*That's* what they say they gonna give us back!"

"How big is it, the land they're giving back?" I asked.

"Two kilometer. That's all. Two kilometer each way. Back then they took a million kilometer. Now they gonna give us *two* kilometer back! All around it, all around that matchbox, they gonna keep diggin' their holes. We can't go there, outside of that matchbox. That's still theirs. That's lease land, crown land, they say. That don't belong to us anymore, they say. We can't go around there this way and that way. We gotta stay inside our matchbox, they tell us. Right there, in that little place in there, inside that matchbox. Outside of there they say we can't hunt kangaroo. Can't fish there. Can't make fires there. Can't hunt goanna there. Can't even visit our sacred places there!

"They say they gonna make a national park out of all that after they stop diggin' their holes. But we don't want a national park! We want our land back! Not a matchbox with holes all around it!"

She stabbed her cane tip repeatedly and angrily at the parched red earth around the inner rectangle.

"See? That's it! Nothin' but holes! They killed the land with their holes! Just go around everywhere leavin' holes. That's what they do, those white people. Dig up the rivers. Dig up the mountain. Dig up all the trees and throw 'm away like rubbish. Then after it's all dead, after they through makin' all their holes in that land, they gonna make a national park there. Make it for the tourists!

"Oh, they're everywhere now, those tourists. When we go up

to the hills, go up to the mountain, go down to the river, always the tourists are there. The tourists are everywhere! They think the land is for them, just for them.

"But that's *our* land! Wandjina gave us that land back in the Dreamtime. That land's who we are! We *are* that country! Without that country we're nobody, we're nothin'. And it can't be just any land, you know? It has to be *that* land!"

WE'RE FOREIGNERS HERE

"Here at Mowanjum, here's where they made us come to live all those years ago. But this isn't our land, our country. It's not Lorrie's land, not my land. This land belongs to Ngarinyin people, not to Wunambal people, not to Worrora people. To us this is a foreign land. We're foreigners here! We don't have our sacred places here. We can't teach our young people here. This is not our tribal land. Our men, our boys, they can't enter the Law here. They got to go back to where our people lived, their own people, their own country. We got Dreamtime stories in it.

"The young boys, they got to do their men's business there so they can become men, full men. Here at Mowanjum they can only be half men. They got to go there to our own country to learn our tribal ways. Otherwise they might get lost in the white man's world. The old men, they got big things to show the young people. They got big Law for all the young boys to enter. That's the only place they can do that Law business. They can't do it here at Mowanjum. This isn't our place.

"Once not long ago we went to visit there, Lorrie and me, up to Mitchell Plateau. We wanted to take our young people there to show them the sacred places so they would know where they are, where they belong. But it's all holes. All holes they dug for their aluminum. People could fall in them. Everywhere there's big holes you could drive a truck through. They never cover it up or plant the trees back. Just leave all the holes. That's their way. Even where the sacred places are, just big holes!

"We was walking around with a thing . . . you know, a sacred thing. I can't tell you its name. The name is secret. It's a . . . a . . . a *thing*, a sacred thing. One of our men, he walked up to one of the holes where the sacred place is supposed to be. The thing, that sacred thing, it flew right out of his hand and fell into the hole. The man started to climb down into the hole to get it back. But something told him not to go down there. Something whistled, you know? It was the spirit people, the people that died long time ago. He heard them whistle and he stopped. It was a warning, that whistle. A warning! The people from before were warning him not to go down there. Once it was a sacred place and now it's only a hole! And out of the hole came that whistling! It's the spirit people, that's who it is. They're lost, they're lonely, they're angry . . . angry at white people, angry at us their own people, angry at everybody because their sacred place is just a hole in the ground now!"

WE REPRESENT GOD'S CREATION

"They even destroyed the plants, those mining people. Those are the plants we're named after. And we're named after the ground, after the trees and after the animals, after the hills and the mountains, even the stars in the sky, even the clouds. We're named after everything that God gave us, you know? In our tribal way we're named after them.

"All these things, the plants and the trees, the mountains and the hills and the stars and the clouds, we *represent* them. You see these trees over there? We represent them. I might represent that tree there. Might be my name there, in that tree. Yes, and the reeds, too, in the waters . . . the frogs and the tadpoles and the fish . . . even the crickets . . . all kinds of things . . . we *represent* them. We represent everything that God gave us . . . or, we say, that *Wandjina* gave us, you know?"

THE WANDJINA

"Who are the Wandjina?" I asked.

"They were my people long long time ago. They're the ones that made the world. That's our religion, our old religion. The religion from before. Now we got new religion, white people's religion. But our people, they had religion before the missionaries came, you know? And we still have it. But now we go to church to worship the real God in Heaven, like the missionaries tell us to do.

"But we still worship the Wandjina. Just like we worship the God in Heaven. The missionaries, maybe they get mad, but we do it anyway. I was born at the mission, Kunmunya Mission, up in the north. That was 1922. We, my family, we lived in a camp there, lived in a humpy, a hut. My parents taught me all about the bush life, taught me how to hunt kangaroo, how to hunt goanna. And they taught me about the Wandjina. They showed me the Wandjina who live in the caves.

"They taught me everything and I believed them. I was proud. Sometimes I would go up in the cave and lay on my back and look up at the Wandjina, and he would look down at me. He still remembers me, I know. And I still remember him. He waits for me. He waits for my people there in the cave. Only now we can't go up there to him anymore. We can't get up there to that cave and see the Wandjina anymore. He's lonely, that Wandjina. And our old people from long long ago, the spirit people, they up there waitin' for us, too. They looking after us, like the Wandjina. They watching, watching, watching. Watching out for us, just like the Wandjina. He's watching for his people to come back to him so he won't be so lonely. That's what my parents taught me.

"So when they took me to school at the mission, the teacher started tellin' us about the God from Heaven who made the world, you know? And I went back and tell my parents. I said to them, 'There can't be two gods who both made the world. So which is the real God, the Wandjina up there in the cave or the God up there in Heaven?'

"And my parents told me, 'They're the same those two. The God in Heaven and the Wandjina in the cave are the same. Jesus was a Wandjina. But the white people, they call him God. The God in Heaven and the Wandjina in the cave, they're the same, they're one. And Jesus, too. They're all Wandjina, they all made the world.'

"So we believe both, you see. The missionaries told us Wandjina was good until Jesus come along. Wandjina brought the people to Christianity, they said, so Wandjina is good, but you have to set him aside now for the real God in Heaven.

"But we never set Wandjina aside, not really. And he never set us aside. Now we call Jesus Wandjina, and we call God Wandjina, too."

"Are there many Wandjina or one Wandjina?"

"Both," Daisy said. "There's many Wandjina and there's one Wandjina. Just like Jesus and the God in Heaven and that Holy Ghost. Three, but still they're one. So that's like Wandjina, too. Many, but he's still one. He's in the Heaven now with the one God. They're the same. Just the same. Wandjina and the one God. All the same."

THE MISSIONARIES HAD obviously done their work. And the Aboriginal people had adapted, merging the original beliefs and the imported beliefs in their own unique way, different from place to place, from person to person. Whereas the Aboriginal man in Wyndham had given up both belief systems, "blackfella's way" and "Gadia's way," Daisy had embraced both, believed in both, revered both. For her there was no contradiction. Should I blame her for not being "pure" in her beliefs? But what is "purity"? Purity, it seems to me, is in the heart, not the head. It would be hard to imagine anyone purer than Daisy Utemorrah.

An Indian elder in the States once told me: "When White Man came here he sent the missionaries to conquer us. They wanted to convert the Indian people, but they were damn smart. They never converted *all* of us. That wasn't their aim. They always just converted *some* of us. Made some of us Christians while the others followed the traditional ways. That way they knew we would always fight among ourselves, so we could never be strong. That's how they tried to conquer us—and they're still at it today."

WHITE PEOPLE DON'T SAY HELLO

Daisy seemed tired, and we rose to go.

"I'm glad you came to see me," she said. "Not many white people come here, you know. They just pass by. They don't see us. We don't exist for them. They never say hello.

"When you write your book, please tell them. Just be friendly and talk to us and stay with us. Just stop by and say hello to us, that's all we ask.

"We like white people to be friendly, you know? But when they pass us, we think, Oh, he don't care about black people. Your friend Mike here, that's why we like him. He's a good man. Whenever he drives by here, he always comes over to see us and says hello to us, sits down with us and we have a bit of a yarn, you know? We see him in his heart. We see his face. We see his eyes. And we say, 'Oh, he's a good man that Mike Osborn, he's a good people.' If only all the white people could be like that!

"You know, maybe they be smart if they stop by and talk to us. Maybe they learn somethin' from us. A while ago a big fire was comin' up this way. Comin' through the grass and burnin' things up. Some tourist people come by in their caravan and didn't stop to talk to us, just went by like we aren't here, you know? We see them but they don't see us. They don't look. They go down there to the creek to set up their camp. We woulda told them, 'too many flies to go camp down there. And maybe that fire it come getcha.' But they don't want to talk to us black people, and they go down there anyway. Well, we say, 'Let 'm go if that's what they want.'

"But then we see the smoke comin' up this way and they probably don't know about it. They down there sleepin' by the creek, and if they don't get out maybe they gonna burn up. So we send one of the trucks to go down there to the creek and tell 'm, warn 'm, you know? Oh, my, they was very surprised. They just jumped up outa their beds and rolled up their things in a hurry, took their caravan and everything and came up here to our camp. We all stayed there together for the night. They was safe now. The fire swept right through their camp. Then in the morning they went and they see the ground burned where they was staying. Oh, they was very very lucky people. If we wasn't there and they didn't have warning, they been burnt all up like the grass.

"We tell 'm, 'Next time maybe you better stop and say hello to us.' And I think they will. I hope they will.

"So that's what I say you oughta tell 'm in your book. Tell 'm, Just stop by and say hello! That's all we ask."

WANDJINA FIGURE FLOATING ON A CAVE WALL IN THE KIMBERLEY

A Visit to the Wandjina

WE HEADED EAST out of Derby along a broad red-dirt track that cuts like a raw wound through the wilds of the northern Kimberley. The washboard corrugations in the hard-packed dirt set everything in the car to clattering wildly.

"Got to keep your speed up to seventy-eighty k's an hour or more and try to ride the summits of the corrugations," Mike said, expounding his philosophy of negotiating these bone-jolting outback tracks. "That's the smoothest way. Go any slower and the bangs 'n bumps'll only be worse. I've driven roads so bad the cans of Coke in the back of the car'll rub against each other till they finally wear right through and explode. Makes a bloody mess, I'll tell you."

For hours we drove through a stultifying sameness of flat scrublands, seemingly endless kilometers of weirdly shaped termite mounds and stunted gum and wattle trees with an occasional kapok putting out its fiercely yellow blossoms from yawning pods. Here and there wondrous boab trees, almost human in their individuality, gave sudden life to the landscape—some squat and as massive as sumo wrestlers, others as sinuous and slim as prima ballerinas. The land seemed nine-tenths sky—a hot, brazen sky that seemed not to vault overhead but to press down like a heavy hand, suffocating everything beneath.

Here in the Kimberley's antipodean otherland, the seasons oscillate between a steamy tropical Wet, when more than a foot of rain falls in a typical month, and a brain-poaching Dry, when temperatures routinely push into the forties C—100° to 115° F— for months on end. Heat-crazed locals "go troppo"—like a fellow Mike mentioned who had recently set a series of brushfires, proclaiming them to be "signal-fires for UFOs."

"Usually happens around Christmastime. Temps'll hit forty-five degrees. Not a cloud or raindrop for three bloody months. Melts a bloke's mind. People start waitin' for rain, lookin' up at the sky with blank eyes. Sometimes you see lightnin' in the distance, but it seems forever before that first raindrop falls. Then, when it finally comes, usually in January—*whew!* You never saw rains and thunder and lightning like that, mate. Rivers and billabongs start to overflow their banks, and soon half the landscape is underwater. It's like a moving inland sea. Temps cool down to maybe thirty-two, thirty-four degrees, real comfy. Then, when the waters subside, everything turns green for a few weeks and the wildflowers pop like fireworks outa the ground! Few weeks later the heat starts buildin' up, and everything's all scorched again."

Millions of years of alternating Wets and Drys have cracked, scoured, and fissured the Kimberley landscape, exposing rocks more than 3 billion years old in some places and revealing immense deposits of gold, diamonds, uranium, zinc, iron, bauxite, and other mineral treasures. A gold rush around Halls Creek in the 1880s brought the first permanent white settlers to the Kimberley, soon followed by pioneer stockmen who drove their herds thousands of miles cross-country and divided the region's geographical immensity into million-acre cattle stations, virtual empires unto themselves.

Within a few decades most of the local Aboriginal peoples were usurped from their ancestral lands, many dying from white man's diseases, others killed outright or scattered to missions, cattle stations, remote camps, and isolated towns as fringe-dwellers. Of the mere 50,000 or so people living today in this California-size region, perhaps a third are Aboriginals.

The land in places has been almost entirely depopulated. Along many outback tracks you can drive hundreds of kilometers without seeing a single habitation, a single human being, only perhaps an occasional vehicle dragging its gritty plume of red dust through the desolate emptiness.

Here and there low mountains of raw, red sandstone and silver-gray limestone—the remnants of a barrier reef some 350 million years old—erupt out of the terrible monotony of the bush. For all its geological antiquity, the landscape somehow looks temporary, the rubble of ages strewn about in utter disorder. Some colossal accident seems to have happened here. You have a sense of traveling through a vast construction site abandoned by its workers. It seems unfinished—as if the Ancestor Beings will surely be returning momentarily to complete their handiwork.

WE CAMPED THAT night beside a billabong.

"No salties here?" I asked Mike.

I was referring to the huge, massive-jawed saltwater crocodiles, some growing sixteen feet long or more, that often swim scores of kilometers from the sea up estuaries and rivers, occasionally getting stranded in billabongs when the Wet-season floods subside. Though much less common inland than the smaller, slender-snouted freshwater crocs, which may snatch a dog or calf or wallaby but rarely make more than a lacerating swipe at human beings, these grimly smiling man-eaters are the true terrors of the Kimberley.

"Always got to keep an eye out for 'm," Mike said. "But not

likely you'll see any of 'm this far inland. Mebbe a freshie or two. No worries, mate."

In the distance something howled mournfully.

"Dingo," Mike said.

"They ever bother you?"

"You'll probably never see one. They don't much care for people."

The billabong resonated with life-sounds—chirps and whistles, thrums and rasps, gurgles and suspicious ripplings. A warm yet cooling breeze ruffled the heavy night air. In the upper branches of a silver-trunked ghost gum, a raucous flock of white cockatoos settled and resettled nervously.

Not twenty feet away a knee-high goanna—an almost Disney-esque long-necked monitor lizard—stood on its hind legs staring our way. I could have sworn its beady eyes caught mine. A moment later I looked back and it was gone.

"No Dreamtime story for this place?" I asked Mike.

"Probably, but can't say I know it."

After dinner our conversation turned to Mike's early days as a pitcher for a semipro baseball team in Perth.

"Those were *my* Dreamtime days, mate. Had a helluva fast ball, pretty good curve and change-up. An American business-man saw me play, liked my style. Had contacts with the Chicago Cubs, he said. Told me he could arrange a baseball scholarship in the States. I was only sixteen. Trouble was, I'd also been offered a fauna warden's job with the government. They'd had four hundred applicants and chose me. It was a real opportunity, somethin' I'd dreamed of. So I had to pick between dreams. Toughest decision of my life. I decided to take the warden's job, but sometimes I wonder. Maybe it was a big mistake. Now my dream's to explore America outback style . . . and see the bloody World Series!"

He'd served the government for nearly twenty years, the last ten as the only wildlife officer in the Kimberley.

"Spent a lot of my time trackin' poachers. Croc poachers. Fish poachers. Bird smugglers. I loved it. Lots of times I had run-ins with Aboriginals, but I always played fair with 'm. Won their respect. Got to know 'm . . . and they got to know me. They gave me the nickname Turkeyfoot. I had this knack, see, of creepin' up on 'm in the bush without bein' heard or seen, just suddenly poppin' up in their midst . . . sort o' like the wild turkey does, you know? You don't see it, and then suddenly it's there, and then just as suddenly it's gone again, disappeared. I'm bloody proud o' that name!"

After retiring from the service in 1988, he'd started an outback safari business called Kimberley Vision out of Kununurra, supplementing his income by catching rogue crocs on contract from the government.

"That was my second toughest decision—leavin' the service. It wasn't the work, I always loved that. It was the bloody bureaucrats in Perth always meddlin', always tellin' me what to do and what not to do, blokes who wouldn't know a king brown from a coil o' rope!"

His reference was to the king brown snake, one of the deadliest reptiles in the world. "They don't just strike once like most snakes," Mike had told me. "They'll come up and rat-a-tat-tat-tat, bite you ten, twenty times before you even see 'm. You'll likely be dead in a few minutes, mate."

"Any king browns out here?" I asked, eyeing the liquid darkness of the billabong.

"You bet. They're probably here, all right. But, like I say, no worries. They won't bother us."

"How do you know?"

He wiped a smile from his lips with the back of his hand.

"To tell you the truth, Harv, I don't. But I've been swagging out here all these years, and I'm still here to talk about it, right?"

A TOUGH-MINDED REALIST, this Mike Osborn. Level-headed to a fault. His competence in matters of survival and good sense both amazed and humbled me. He was the perfect guide, the perfect companion. Though twenty years my junior, he treated me with a fatherly toleration and bemused concern, smiling wanly at my fears and imaginings. Many a time, stumbling up a rocky scree or clinging to a narrow ledge, I felt myself losing my balance only to sense the steadying grasp of his hand in mine and a calming "Easy there, mate. You'll make it."

His Fu Manchu mustache gave his movie-handsome face an appropriately ferocious aspect for a veteran "bushie." He'd reluctantly trimmed it at my impertinent suggestion during our trip the year before, revealing an underlying countenance as wholesome as a Norman Rockwell Boy Scout's. He'd hated it.

"Just ain't me," he'd snarled, looking unhappily in a mirror. "The blokes'd laugh me outa the pub." Within a couple of weeks the full-length mustachio had returned.

And yet I've known few men kinder or more considerate. Beneath that crusty macho exterior beats a sentimentalist's noble heart. Dozens of times during the 35,000-odd kilometers we've driven together, I've seen him come to the aid of stranded travelers, stopping for hours to jury-rig someone's broken axle or fix a rope to haul a broken-down vehicle back to the nearest roadhouse.

I remember the night we were driving along a lonely stretch of road south of Broome. Our headlights picked out some shadowy figures waving at us in the road.

"Could be trouble," I said, having heard of unwary travelers being mugged by groups of drunken youths.

"No worry, mate. We'll see what's the problem."

We stopped, and the group of shadowy figures approached the car. In the darkness they seemed definitely menacing.

"Just a family of Aboriginals," Mike reassured me. "Looks like their truck's conked out."

Sure enough, he was right. The family of eight or nine Aboriginals had been waiting for hours for the next car to come along. Mike worked at their vehicle for forty-five minutes, finally deciding it was "no go." After all but emptying our larder of provisions and passing them out to the grateful family, we roped their front bumper to the rear of our Land Ranger and pulled them all the way back to town, more than fifty kilometers out of our way.

"Outback etiquette." Mike shrugged as we headed back.

Another time we were tooling along an outback track when a flock of birds suddenly wheeled low out of the sky directly across our path. I'd many times seen Mike slow down, even swerve to avoid hitting birds or other animals in the road. But this time one of the birds hit our front window with deadly impact. Instantly Mike braked the car, threw it into reverse, and backed up a hundred yards or so in a cloud of red dust.

"Have to make sure it's dead," he said. "Damn, but I hate myself when I hit one of 'm."

Jumping out of the car, he searched the brush.

"Here she is, she's still alive," he called.

He returned with the trembling creature, still fluttering weakly, cradled in his hands.

"Crested pigeon," he said, setting it in my lap. "Here, you take her while I drive. Hold her gentle around the wings, mate. Maybe we can take her home and get her well."

The bird was surprisingly warm in my hands. I could feel the beating of its heart.

"My God, it's beautiful," I murmured.

Its little head had a spiky crest of silvery feathers, each exquisitely formed with marvelously intricate interweaving patterns. Its body feathers were a lovely mother-of-pearl, almost iridescent. And its eyes . . . I had never seen such eyes, concentric circles of yellow and brown within an outer circle of brilliant, pulsating orange-red. I cupped my hands carefully around its wings to keep them from flapping.

But the bird struggled, terrified.

"Here, you take it," I said, feeling helpless.

Mike took the bird in his hands and held it maternally to his chest, softly stroking its back.

Still it struggled. Then, after a few agonizing seconds, it gave a convulsive jerk and went still. A greenish gray nictitating membrane slowly slid over those lovely eyes with their glistening, pulsating concentric circles.

"She's had it, mate," Mike said softly.

He carried the now-limp body back to the side of the road and set it on the ground, covering it with brush.

"Dingo'll take care of it," he said, swallowing the crack in his voice.

We headed back up the road in funereal silence.

"You never get used to these things," he finally said.

NOW, AFTER A delicious meal of lamb stew cooked in an Aboriginal-style pit fire, I unstrapped and rolled out my swag—an inch-thin mattress wrapped about by a heavy canvas tarp with two flaps that can be pulled loosely shut to provide a modicum of protection against wind, cold, or rain. Mike was already sprawled out on his swag, snoring softly—pitching a no-hitter in some Dreamtime World Series, no doubt—and I was left to my own imaginings. I pulled the canvas flaps of my swag over my chest and stared up into the night sky. The Milky Way trailed across my field of vision like a twisted bridal veil of incandescent blue-white gas. Low on the horizon the Southern Cross hung pendant, reminding me of a gleaming crucifix intruding into the Aboriginal sky. My mind took flight into those stars, tracking the ghostly footprints of the Ancestor Beings on their celestial wanderings.

Someone—something—laughed aloud in the darkness.

"Kookaburra?" I called over to Mike.

He never answered.

And I didn't care.

WE AWOKE WITH the flies and quickly broke camp.

"There's a cave not far from here I want to show you," Mike announced. "One of my 'secret places.' It's around back and up the side of one of those cliffs out there. A big rock overhang with old paintings of the Wandjina. The Aboriginals seem to have forgotten all about it. Hasn't been touched for years so far as I can tell. Hold your hat! We're takin' a little ride!"

He swerved the Land Ranger off the red-dirt track, and we were off, bouncing wildly through a yellow blur of high cane grass whose seed heads rattled like buckshot against the windshield. Shattered cane stalks quickly covered the vehicle's front end, completely blocking Mike's view and forcing him to stick his head out the side window to see where he was going, which seemed to me to be absolutely nowhere. We lurched and jounced through a slalom of gum and wattle trees, narrowly missing scores of concrete-hard, chest-high termite mounds.

"Where the hell are we going?" I asked, desperately bracing myself to keep my head from banging against the roof of the car.

"Shortcut!" he announced.

At last, when it seemed we must be totally lost, we came to a barely recognizable track tunneling through the thick brush. This we followed for a few minutes, then plowed back through more high grass. The pattern repeated. I began to realize that there was an almost invisible network of tracks out here, a web of pathways discernible only to the practiced eye.

"You've been this way before?" I asked.

"Nope."

"Then how do you know there's a track out there?"

"You get a feel for it. There's always a track. Hard to find sometime, but it's always there."

"Always?"

"Always."

"Aboriginal tracks?"

"What else?"

"Dreaming tracks?"

"I suppose, mate. Maybe once. Now they're just tracks for bloody anyone."

WE FINALLY REACHED the base of some low, red cliffs and parked the Land Ranger.

"Up this way," Mike said. "Watch your step."

We scrambled up a stony path among large strewn boulders to a rock overhang and ducked beneath. The red sandstone walls and ceiling were covered with a ghostly gallery of large, white-painted faces, wide-eyed and mouthless, staring down at us as if startled by our arrival.

These were the Wandjina, or Cloud-Beings, of whom Daisy Utemorrah had spoken—uniquely haunting rock-art paintings found only in the central and west Kimberley. Mike had shown me several other Aboriginal rock-art sites in the east Kimberley, but in those the sinuous Rainbow Snake had been the dominant figure, surrounded by a panoply of red-ocher turtles, crocodiles, lizards, sticklike hunters with spears, and fright-figures called "devil-men."

Archeologists have dated some of the Rainbow Serpent paintings to 9000 B.C. or earlier, which, according to Josephine Flood in her *Archaeology of the Dreamtime,* "would make the Rainbow Serpent myth the longest continuing religious belief documented in the world."

Even older Aboriginal rock drawings in South Australia have recently been dated back to 43,000 B.C., predating by more than

10,000 years the Neolithic cave paintings of Spain and Germany—
hitherto considered the oldest in the world.

But these Wandjina figures of the Kimberley—some of them
carbon-dated at "only" 8,000 years old, twice the age of Egypt's
pyramids—are utterly unlike any other rock paintings elsewhere
in Australia in style and psychological impact. They seem to be
the work of an entirely different mentality and artistic tradition.
Scholars have been chary of attributing them to so "primitive" a
people as Australia's Aboriginals, speculating that they were the
work of ancient Hindus, Egyptians, even the Lost Tribes of
Israel. One pseudoscholar, Erich Von Däniken, in his controver-
sial tome *Chariots of the Gods: Unsolved Mysteries of the Past*, went so
far as to attribute the Wandjina figures to beings from outer
space—interpreting the halolike fringes around their staring
countenances as space helmets.

To local Aboriginal peoples, however, the halos fringing the
faces of the Wandjina figures represent clouds and lightning. For
generations beyond counting, they periodically visited these
caves of the Wandjina to retouch or completely repaint their fading images, believing that by so doing they assured the return of
the life-giving Wet. To them, these Wandjina figures aren't paintings at all; rather, they are the actual living images of the Cloud-
Beings themselves, embedded in the rock for all eternity.

With the near-depopulation of the region's Aboriginal peoples
over the past century, the Wandjina caves—like those of the
Rainbow Snake and other Dreamtime Ancestor Beings—are no
longer retouched, and they grow fainter and more weathered
with each passing year. An attempt by the government in the late
1980s to have some Law Men retouch them resulted in a bitter
outcry among Aboriginal traditionalists who insisted no one any
longer possessed the requisite knowledge to do so. The attempt
was abandoned.

But the Aboriginal art tradition continues, ever transforming itself, in the modern bark paintings and canvases sold for upscale prices in galleries around the world (and for which the Aboriginal artists, alas, rarely receive more than a comparative pittance). New styles continually emerge, clearly demonstrating the extraordinarily resilient artistic genius of Aboriginal people—arguably the world's first artists—and making it, hopefully, no longer necessary for the doubting Gadia mind to attribute these wondrous Wandjina figures to ancient Egyptians or visiting spacemen.

BENEATH THE ENIGMATIC wide-eyed stares of the Wandjina figures, I sat on a ledge of rock and looked out over the almost surreal Kimberley landscape—ranges of fractured red mountains interspersed with shimmering hard-scrub plains. So beautiful from up here, so oppressively monotonous at times when seen from the road below. Far on the horizon I could see a single small flotilla of black-bellied clouds drifting in from the Timor Sea, belching lightning. It takes no great leap of the imagination to picture the Wandjina and other Ancestor Beings on their immemorial travels down there, creating and re-creating the Dreamtime landscape.

Mike interrupted my thoughts.

"Hey, look at this."

He directed my gaze to a shallow trough in the rock ledge; sitting on it were two almost perfectly round polished stones.

"Grinding stones," he said, picking one up and juggling it in his hand like a baseball. I half-expected him to pitch it out on a wicked curve into the abyss, but he set it reverently back in place.

"How old are they?"

"No idea. Maybe a few decades. Maybe centuries. And look here"—he gestured to the stone-littered floor of the cave—"see those stone chips? Some bloke made himself a spear point up here. And this one—see the polished edge?—that's a scraper. Stone Age stuff."

"And what's this?" I asked, picking up what appeared to be a petrified walnut.

"Quandong," Mike answered. "Aboriginals call 'm emu apples. That's just the pit you're lookin' at. You can eat the flesh around 'm when they're ripe. Aboriginal ladies still gather 'm in season. Bitter—pretty awful-tastin', really—but they'll keep a body alive."

"Maybe I'll take it for a Dreamtime souvenir."

"Sorry. Can't take anythin', mate. Not allowed. That's the law—*whitefella's* law, I mean."

Here I was, taking what wasn't mine again. Properly chastised, I set it down.

It was getting unbearably hot. Clouds of flies droning in the cave set up a resonant hum. At least a hundred of them had settled on the sweaty back of Mike's shirt. Reaching around to pat my own back, I raised hundreds more into the air.

We climbed down to the car for the long drive back to Kununurra, Mike's hometown in the east Kimberley, where he had arranged an appointment for us the next morning with the elders of the local Aboriginal community.

CAMP

Pelican

Dreaming

3

THE LONE MALE voice drifted out of the sky, a mystic tenor rever-
berating off the slabs of red sandstone tilting gigantically around
us as we climbed the rough-hewn stone steps up Kelly's Knob to
an overlook above the Aboriginal community of Waringarri.

"What's that? Some kind of ceremony going on?" I called up to
Mike, who was nimbly step-hopping over boulders ahead of me.

"No idea, mate. . . . Sounds familiar somehow."

The voice was piercing, haunting, almost supernaturally loud.
It seemed to be coming from just the other side of Kelly's Knob.

"That's Waringarri right over there," Mike said as we approached
the overlook. "Must be comin' from there."

"*Ah-yahhh . . . Aahhh . . . Aahhhh . . . ,*" went the voice, cutting the
air like a thin surgical wire.

"*Yahhh . . . Aahhh . . . Aahhhhhhh. . . .*"

Now it took on a breathy deep-stomached rhythm.

"*ðu-DUH-ðu-ree-loonggg, ðu-DUH-ðu-ree-loonggg. . . .*"

And now the hoarsely thrumming drone of a didgeridoo—that
most soul-wrenching of Aboriginal musical instruments—joined
in, followed by the sharp clickings of clapsticks. The sounds of

human voice, didgeridoo, and clapsticks intertwined with magical syncopated effect. I envisioned looking down from the edge of the overlook and seeing a gyrating circle of white-and-red-daubed devotees dancing wildly to the ancient Aboriginal rhythms. We might have been stumbling onto a corroboree of the Ancestor Beings themselves.

"Yothu Yindi!" Mike called back on reaching the overlook.

"What's that?" I asked, scrambling after him.

"Rock group. Aboriginal rock group. Comin' from the loudspeakers down there at Waringarri. Must be on the community radio."

My Dreamtime vision evaporated. The music drifted up, almost surreal, suddenly joined now by the hard modern beat of non-Aboriginal drums and electric guitars.

"Well, I heard it on the radio," sang out the lead voice, *"and I saw it on the television. Back in 1988. All those talking politicians."*

The words resounded off the rock walls of the natural sandstone amphitheater around us.

"Words are easy, words are cheap. Much cheaper than our priceless land. But promises can disappear, just like writing in the sand."

"What's their name again?" I asked Mike.

"Yothu Yindi," he repeated. "One of the best-known rock groups in the country."

"Treaty yeah. Treaty now. Treaty yeah. Treaty now."

The guttural wail of the didgeridoo echoed eerily.

We looked down at Waringarri, a low sprawl of tin-roofed buildings set amidst scraggly gum trees at the foot of Kelly's Knob.

"Aboriginals call this hill Mirima, not Kelly's Knob," Mike explained. "Means 'Pelican Dreaming,' I think."

"Another sacred site?"

"Of course. The whole bloody land's a sacred site, mate."

The words of Yothu Yindi rang out as if in confirmation: *"This land was never given up. This land was never bought and sold."*

"You can feel it if you try," Mike went on. "Like Kelly's Knob here. There's somethin' special about it . . . call it sacred if you like. One of my favorite places in all the world. Come up here from time to time to have a think. Does a soul good."

"Treaty yeah. Treaty now. Treaty yeah. Treaty now." came Yothu Yindi's final refrain.

The pounding rock rhythms stopped abruptly, and out of the sudden silence came a contrapuntal chorus of birdsong.

"Just listen to those birds!" Mike enthused. "Hear 'm? That one's a magpie lark . . . and there's a gray currawong . . . oh, and there's a willie wagtail . . . and that one, that's a bowerbird."

"What's that one circling up there?" I asked, pointing to a wheeling silhouette high above our heads.

"Fork-tailed kite."

A bloody ornithologist's paradise, this place. Birds everywhere, singing out of the Dreamtime.

"Any pelicans up here?"

"Naw. Not this high. They keep 'mselves down by the river mostly. See plenty of 'm down on the Ord by the low-water bridge at Ivanhoe Crossing."

MIKE SET UP his tripod and camera to capture the lavender dusk settling over the wide-angled landscape—Waringarri directly below us, the tidy administrative center and tourist town of Kununurra just off to the left, the black-dirt fields of the Ord River Irrigation Project stretching flat to the mountained horizon, intersected by sun-glazed canals. Far to the west another sandstone massif thrust up in lone splendor from the visionary topography.

"That's called Sleeping Buddha," Mike said.

"What's the Aboriginal name?"

"No idea. But you can be sure it's got one."

"And a Dreamtime story, too, no doubt."

"No doubt."

He focused his lens on Waringarri, which was fading into shadows a few hundred feet below. Lights were coming on in a few of the windows, winking alluringly.

"People don't see it," Mike commented.

"Don't see what?"

"Waringarri I'm talkin' about. The Aboriginal community down there. Tourists come through Kununurra by the tens o' thousands every year. Truckies float through, government blokes, all kinds o' people. But they just don't see it. Maybe a few stop by the art gallery to buy an Aboriginal painting at a steal. But all those other buildings and the people livin' there? They might as well be invisible. The only Aboriginals visitors remember are the ones pissed on grog outside the pubs in town, staggerin' around the streets causin' trouble, doin' humbug. That's the way they think all Aboriginals are."

I knew the syndrome. Whitefella's blindness. Eyeless in an Aboriginal Gaza. Seeing but not seeing. Looking through or past or around but never *at*. Expecting nothing and invariably finding it. Seeing no one and so never meeting anyone. Remember Daisy Utemorrah's plea: "Just stop by and say hello. That's all we ask."

I myself had been guilty, eyeless as any.

I remember the day two years before when Mike and I, coming up from Perth, drove into a desert town in south-central Western Australia. It was my first trip to the outback. I had seen a few Aboriginal people in Perth, mostly street loiterers, but nothing could have prepared me for this place.

We'd been swagging out for days, and I was saturated to the soul with red dust and grit. My city-soft muscles ached for a real bed and a hot shower.

Mike recalled a hotel in the little town. "Not much really, but it's got rooms."

"Doesn't have to be fancy," I said.

"Won't be. No worries there, mate. You book yourself a room if you like. Me, I'll swag out in the desert on the edge of town, meet you for breakfast in the morning."

"Think they'll have hot water?" I asked.

His eyes studied me with benign contempt.

"Good chance. Double-check before you book in."

The town itself seemed hardly more substantial than a mirage, a ghostly distillation of dust, shadow, and fading sunlight. Its rusted tin sheds and sagging plank buildings converged on the utterly bleak main intersection. On one corner of the intersection a peeling sign on a swaybacked two-story building announced HOTEL. The second-floor windows were boarded up.

"That's it?" I asked as we approached.

"Nope. Hasn't been a hotel there for years. Only the first-floor pub's open. The new hotel is down the street, through that alleyway and out back."

We parked the car and walked into a scene that might have been the stage set for an expressionistic ballet—a tableau of despair with dozens of Aboriginal men and women lurching, staggering, some sprawled, some prone, some slumped in doorways, some on their knees or haunches with arms outstretched in perpetual supplication to the few passersby. Small children played lethargically among them, eyes crawling with flies, noses crusted with snot. Literally thousands of empty beer cans lay strewn about the street and sidewalks. The stink of alcohol, vomit, and piss was unmistakable and utterly sickening. It seemed hard to believe such a place could exist. I was reeling in shock.

We made one pass up the main street and back, stepping cautiously among the murmuring bodies, kicking beer cans out of our way. Mike showed me the way to the new hotel, but I raised a hand in protest.

"To hell with the hot bath. Let's get out of here. We can swag out somewhere . . . anywhere."

"Thought you'd feel that way, mate. Can't say I disagree."

We picked our way back to the car and, to my vast relief, made good our escape.

NOW, LOOKING DOWN on Waringarri from the height of Kelly's Knob—Pelican Dreaming—I realized I had to blink away my own eyelessness. I could no longer look away. Next morning we would be walking in there, and I could feel self-doubt gnawing again in the pit of my stomach. Would I be able to see my way past the wall of grog to meet the Dreamkeepers I'd envisioned?

Surely the drunks and the Dreamkeepers couldn't be one and the same?

I remember that stranded Aboriginal family in the conked-out truck that Mike had so graciously rescued that dark night south of Broome. Among them had been an elderly man with a full white beard and a sweetly genial face, seemingly the epitome of wisdom. Jocko was his name. A fount of Dreamtime stories, no doubt. He'd been quite drunk, a huge disappointment to me. I spoke to him only briefly, asking him how old he was.

He looked at me.

"Younger'n *you'll* ever be, mate!" he chirped, grinning.

Mike found that hilarious.

Aboriginal wisdom, indeed.

"Gotta learn to see beyond the fumes," Mike said. "Just 'cause a bloke gets pissed now and again doesn't mean he's not wise when he's off the grog. People have their wet and dry seasons, too."

ALTHOUGH WARINGARRI SEEMED prosperous enough compared with some other Aboriginal communities I'd passed through, the power of grog, I knew, still gripped many of its people. I'd seen them outside the pubs of Kununurra, walking aimlessly or sitting in groups on the wide grass median strip along the main high-way—lanky, bare-chested youths with sullen eyes, gnarled old men and women, all of them raggedly dressed, barefoot, their faces masks of pain and desperation. Nothing as extreme as that desert town down south, perhaps, but still a haunting reminder of some terrible loss to the human spirit. The Gadia pass them by. Unseeing. Eyeless.

"Just stop by and say hello. That's all we ask."

Daisy Utemorrah's message rang in my conscience.

TED CARLTON, MIRIWOONG:

"I'm an Aboriginal, I'm an Australian, I'm a Miriwoong."

Beat the Grog

4

"HEAR, YOU MOB!" announced chairman Ted Carlton to the assembled elders of Waringarri. "This here bloke from America says he got somethin' to say, so we're lettin' him say it so we all can hear."

I was seated on a wooden chair at the center of the main meeting room of the Waringarri Aboriginal Corporation—governing body for the Miriwoong, Gadjerong, and other peoples of the east Kimberley at Kununurra.

Several dozen pairs of Aboriginal eyes focused on me hard, looking right through me. I had the distinct sensation of being X-rayed.

"So listen up, I say," Ted Carlton continued. "He's an *Awtha* who wrote this book you're passin' around here about American Indians. Says he wants to write a book about Aboriginal people."

He turned to me. "OK, mate, go ahead. Have your say. We're listenin'."

If I'd had a hat in my hands, I'd have wrung it. I dislike these kinds of situations.

"Thanks for listening."

I heard myself speak as if from a distance.

"I'm here to ask your help."

The tittering in the room subsided. Those Aboriginal eyes bored into my Gadia soul.

"You write this book here?" a voice asked.

"Yes."

"Now you writin' about Aboriginal people?"

"Exactly. . . . That's why I'm here."

"You lookin' for Dreamtime stories?"

"No . . . not necessarily. . . . Whatever you care to share with my readers."

"Mmmm." A general murmur went through the room.

"If anyone here would like to talk with me, I'm ready to listen."

"So who wants to talk to this bloke?" asked Ted.

Silence.

More tittering.

"How about Griffo?" came a tentative voice.

"Righto, Griffo's the one!" someone seconded.

An elderly man rose, shaking his head.

"That's old Griffo," Mike whispered.

Griffo made a beeline out of the room.

Laughter.

"OK, you mob," said Ted. "Anyone else?"

Again silence.

Ted looked at me.

"They're shy," he said. "Leave your book, and let 'm think it over. Come on back see me tomorrow mornin'. *I'll* talk to you anyway, mate."

"DOESN'T LOOK TOO promising," I lamented as we left.

"No worry. They'll come round," Mike counseled. "Like Ted says, they're shy. Takes time. Come on, I'll introduce you to

Barry Carlton over at the radio station. He's the local disc jockey. Lively young bloke. You'll like 'm."

"Ted's brother?"

"Nephew, I think. Lots of people here named Carlton. Their families used to work at Carlton Station years ago. Took the station's name. Came here to live at Kununurra when they started buildin' the dam and irrigation project back in the sixties."

We walked over to the radio station housed in a modern new building across the compound.

Barry Carlton, a bright and effusive young man in his twenties, greeted the Awtha with a warm handshake and engaging smile. He flipped appreciatively through a copy of *Wisdomkeepers*, nodding to himself as he read.

"You find there's many similarities between Indian people and Aboriginal people?" he asked.

"That's why I'm here," I explained. "A Mohawk chief named Jake Swamp told me, 'Go over there and talk to those Aboriginal people, too. Those guys are doin' over there what we're doin' over here. It's the same thing.'"

"How's it the same?" Barry asked, obviously intrigued by the parallel.

"Indians," I explained, "were conquered by the same people who came here. To them the land is the number-one thing, same as with Aboriginal people. When they lost the land they lost their identity. They started to lose their religion, lose their language."

"Yeah, that's the same," Barry concurred. "Sounds like the same Gadia to me. Takin' everythin', givin' back nothin'. They have a Dreamtime, the Indians?"

"Something like it," I said. "The Iroquois and some other tribes, for instance, have what you might call a Turtle Dreaming. They call the North American continent "Great Turtle Island." They believe that when the Creator made the world, he put it on the back of a Turtle. They also have clans named after other animals—the Wolf, the Bear, the Heron, and so on—something like your Pelican Dreaming or Emu Dreaming. White men called it a pagan religion because they thought Indians worshiped the wolf and bear and so on. But Indians never worshiped those animals. They just considered them their ancestors and named their clans after them."

"The same, just the same," Barry repeated. "We don't worship the pelican or any of those animals. They're symbols, not something we worship. We're *related* to those creatures. Our Dreaming is where those animals live. Knowing your Dreaming means you know where you fit in on the land. Take us away from our land and you take us away from our Dreaming."

He pulled out a map of the Kimberley.

"See here, right here around Kununurra . . . this is Pelican Dreaming country. And over here, by Kalumburu, that's Rainbow Snake Dreaming country. Down here, that's Barramundi Dreaming. You know the barramundi, the big fish?"

I nodded. "Sure. Mike here took me fishin' down on the Ord. We caught a few. . . . Maybe we shouldn't have."

"No problem," Barry said. "If it's not your Dreaming it's OK to catch 'm."

He pointed again at the map.

"Now over here to the east, the other side o' Lake Argyle, that's Rainbow Snake country again. That's how it is all over bloody Australia. Everywhere's there's a Dreaming. White people don't understand that. . . . You know that diamond mine up by Lake Argyle? Way I heard it, back in the seventies, some white prospectors found an Aboriginal burial up there, a skeleton and a skull. In the eye socket o' the skull they found a diamond, and that's how they knew there was diamonds there. Now they dug up a whole mountain to get at the diamonds. But that mountain's a sacred place, it's the crossover point of the Rainbow Snake

Dreaming and the Barramundi Dreaming. Now they destroyed the whole mountain. It's not there anymore, just a big hole. How you think that makes us feel? They not only steal the land but then they destroy it . . . just for pieces o' glass!"

"Same thing happened to the Indians in the Black Hills," I said. "Only there the white man dug up the sacred mountains for gold and uranium."

"Yeah, yeah . . . they're after gold and uranium here, too. It's just the same!" Barry said. "So are the Indians gettin' back their land, gettin' back their sovereignty?"

"They're trying," I said. "But I'm afraid they're having a hard time of it. They'd envy your Outstation Movement, I think. Not many of their land claims are succeeding."

Behind Barry, on the wall of his office, hung a flag with a yellow circle centered on broad stripes of red and black.

"That's our flag, the Aboriginal flag," Barry explained. "That shows we're a sovereign people. See, the red stripe is for our blood, all the blood we've shed. And the yellow circle, that's the sun, the giver of life. And the black stripe, that's the black color of our people. . . . I'm bloody proud o' that! Do Indian people have a flag of their own?"

"Not that I know of. Maybe they will one day."

"You wanna talk to our people?" Barry asked. "Talk to 'm on the radio? Tell 'm about Indians? They'd like to hear about that . . . how their Indian brothers are doin'.'"

I mentioned that I'd been interviewed on Indian radio stations in the States.

"They got Indian radio there?"

"You bet. It's very important. A way of communicating they never had before. They're basically an oral culture, just like Aboriginal people. So radio's the perfect medium for them. Chief Jake Swamp up at Akwasasne in New York State runs a station for Mohawk people. The Lakota have a radio station at Pine

Ridge. There are lots of others. It's a way of reaching the people."

"I'd like to meet this Jake Swamp," Barry enthused. "I think we got a lot to talk about!"

"I'll tell him," I said.

We went into the recording studio, and within moments I was wired to headphones and microphones and found myself speaking to an unseen Aboriginal listening audience.

"All right, you mob," Barry began. "We're talkin' here this mornin' with Hardy Harden . . . "

"Errr . . . it's Harvey Arden."

"OK. Harvey Harden."

For twenty minutes or so Barry interviewed me on my travels through Native America and the Indian-Aboriginal parallels he'd found so interesting. I wondered how my nasal voice was coming across, envisioning the Aboriginal people who might be listening in their homes and far-scattered outback camps. At interview's end I invited any of them who cared to be included in the book to get in touch with us through Barry at the radio station or just to come up and talk to us if they saw us on the street.

"OK, you mob, so if you wanna be in sort of a book or just have a yarn with Hardy here, just come on up and talk to 'm if you see 'm around."

"Yeah, please do," I added. "If you see a handsome strapping young 'Crocodile' Dundee type next to a funny-lookin' white bloke with white hair and a gray mustache, that's probably us."

NEXT DAY WE returned to Waringarri to see Ted Carlton.

"Any takers from the meeting?" I asked.

"One fella," Ted said. "Old Jim Ward up at Alligator Hole. Says he'll talk to you if you like."

"That's all?"

"Yup. Only one who offered."

"Oh."

"What about old Griffo?" Mike asked.

"Forget it. He doesn't want to talk. None o' the ladies either. They're shy, like I said. And maybe this isn't the best time. Everyone's busy. Today's pension day. People get their checks. You'll see lots of 'm drunk all over the place . . . not a pretty sight, mate. Maybe you better come back another time . . . though it'll probably be the same then."

Smiling genially at this dispirited Awtha, Ted leaned back in his swivel chair. Although he must have been pushing forty—he had five children, I knew from Mike—he looked hardly out of his twenties, with an expansive hairdo that gave him more the appearance of a rock musician than that of a corporation chairman. A stylishly battered cap sat at a rakish angle atop his long, tousled locks. He propped his sandaled feet among the piled papers on his desk.

"That's mostly what I been doin' around here lately," he said. "Foolin' with all these papers, government forms, questionnaires, applications, more papers, more government forms . . . it's a bloody headache. I gotta help our people with all the paperwork. Can't do it themselves. They come in here, need to fill out the forms for the government to claim a piece of land, get a new house, get a motorcar, get their pensions straightened out. . . . Papers, papers, papers . . . that's Gadia's way, not blackfella's way. . . . Still, I'm chairman, it's my job. Someone's gotta do the dirty work, like fillin' out all these forms."

"And talkin' to prying visitors," I added.

"Bloody right there, mate." He grinned. "So what you blokes wanna know?"

"Whatever you'd like to share," I repeated.

Ted nodded.

"Well, the most important work I do these days is head up the Alcohol Project . . . educate people about the grog. That's the big thing. Till we get 'm off the grog, everything else is for nothin'.

All these young fellas, they're too busy drinkin'. They don't wanna work. Why should they work when they got all this free money comin' in? At least when you're on the grog you can get happy, you can laugh for a while, you can forget for a while.

"I was one of 'm, too, in the past. I don't do that anymore. But I had to work really hard to beat the grog. Lotta people here they're tryin' hard, but the temptation's too strong for 'm. When

I used to be drinkin' there'd be, say, five of us blokes. One day I'd buy the grog, next day the next bloke'd buy it, next day the next. Stay pissed all the time. Went on for years. That's just the way it was.

"We forgot our culture, forgot the Dreamtime. . . . All we remembered was the grog-time.

"So that's what I keep poundin' into these young fellas' heads: *Beat the grog. Beat the grog. We gotta beat the grog.*

"Gotta get outa the grog-time. Gotta get back to the real-time and get back to the Dreamtime, too."

"HERE AT WARINGARRI, this is a big important time for us. We're workin' to overcome these problems. We're learnin' we can do it if we all work together. Workin' together is what Waringarri's all about. Waringarri—it means, like, 'One Big Mob . . . One Big Mob workin' together'!

"All these things are happenin' here. . . . We got a construction company, a building mob. We got an arts and crafts center. We got the radio station. We got the language school to save the old languages. We got job training so our young fellas'll be able to work for their own people. We got the Alcohol Project. We got people like old Jim Ward out at Alligator Hole makin' new camps out in the bush. Things are happenin' like never before.

"It's a good time . . . if only we can *beat the grog!*

"You Gadia, you gotta understand. All these people, young people, old people, you see 'm layin' down in the park, all drunk, all dirty. But you gotta understand. These are *real* people. They're *not* just drunks. Those drunks are really good men!

"I know, I used to work with 'm at Carlton Station. I've mustered cattle and broken horses with all these people. I drove cattle to the meat works in Wyndham with 'm. We used to live on the stations with our families. Grog was no big problem back then. Sure, we got pissed—they used to give each of us four cans of beer when we knocked off work each day. That's how I got into alcohol. But then we just slept it off and went back to work. We had jobs back then, we did our work. Got enough to keep us alive.

"Then the bloody government, back about 1970, when they

decided to finally give us our citizenship rights, they told the station owners they had to pay us the same pay as Gadia blokes. Down in Canberra and Sydney and Melbourne, that sounded good to the Gadia people 'cause they felt guilty for us. But what it meant, how it turned out, was the station owners just made us get out. Kicked us off the stations. If they had to pay us Gadia wages, then they figured they'd just as soon hire Gadias instead o' blackfellas. Besides, by then they were gettin' helicopters and bull buggies to do the musterin'. They got road trains, those big trucks, to do the drovin'. They didn't need us Aboriginal people no more. So we got put off the stations. Not just us but our families, too. No jobs, no homes, no pay, no place to go. Just got put off like you chase away a pack o' dogs.

"So lots of us we came to Kununurra here. Fringe-dwellers they called us. Just hangin' around the edges. Doin' nothin'. Livin' for nothin'. Livin' on the dole. Drownin' in the grog. Goin' from pension check to pension check.

"And that's where Waringarri comes in. At last we're helping ourselves. All these different Aboriginal peoples from all those different places. We're learnin' to come together, to be One Big Mob. That's the only way we can save ourselves.

"We're plannin' to set up an alcohol rehabilitation center way outa town, a place they can go to sober up and learn they can *still* have plenty good fun. If you get 'm off the grog and take 'm out bush, they're different people!

"And that's why I say that, even with all the problems, it's a *good* time for Aboriginal people, a better time than we had for many many years.

"Anyway, you blokes go see Jim Ward up at Alligator Hole. He'll talk with you even if the others won't. Ask 'm about the old days, how it was before in the long time ago."

Before we left, Mike asked Ted one more question. "If you

could say something to people all around the world, give 'm a message from Aboriginal people, so to speak, what would it be, Ted?"

Ted thought a moment, composing himself. "Well, I suppose this is what I'd tell 'm if I could."

He cleared his throat and spoke the following memorable words in the same tone of voice he'd used the day before in addressing the elders:

Hear, you mob!
I'm an Aboriginal.
I'm an Australian.
I'm a Miriwoong.
We're all one family,
All together,
We human beings.
All one big mob!

"Tell 'm that," he said.

JIM WARD, MIRIWOONG:

"The old law, it's never goin' to die."

A New World at Alligator Hole

5

ON OUR WAY out of town the next morning to see Jim Ward at Alligator Hole, an elderly Aboriginal man with a jovial smile waved us down at the petrol station.

"Hey, there's Danny Wallace! A really fine old bloke!" Mike said.

He spoke with the man for a few minutes, then returned to the car.

"Seems old Danny heard you on Waringarri radio the other day. He's a bit shy but says we should come on up to Emu Creek and have a yarn. Wants to meet the Awtha. Says wait a day or two . . . too much grog goin' around right now. Just got their pension checks on Tuesday. Should be lots quieter tomorrow. Says old George Wallaby the Law Man wants to meet you, too."

"Well, maybe we're gettin' somewhere after all."

"Mebbe. Whatever's supposed to happen'll happen."

"That Aboriginal philosophy?"

"Bloody anyone's philosophy, mate."

MIRIWOONG ELDER Jim Ward sat on the bare springs of a rain-rusted iron cot beneath the open sky, surrounded by a panoramic ring of steep red-rock mountains.

"Got to fix a roof for this shed here," Jim explained. "Construction mob from Waringarri laid down this concrete slab for a floor a few days ago, but they left the roof for me to do. Too hot today. Gets an old bloke tired. I asked some of the youngfellas to help, but they're in town doin' humbug. Grog, you know. They don't like doin' the work. Just drinkin', that's what they like."

He gestured toward some sheets of corrugated-iron roofing material lying in disorder on the ground. "Heavy bloody stuff. Takes more'n one man, but I guess I'll manage by myself. Glad to see you blokes, though. Appreciate your comin' out. Gives me a few minutes to sit down and rest these old bones."

"Any way I can give you a hand?" Mike asked.

"Naw . . . that's not why I invited you, mate. You be my guests, you know? Just wanted to talk a bit. Have a yarn for a while, you know? Sorry I got nothin' cold to offer you. So this here's the Awtha?"

"Yeah. . . . Jim Ward, I want you to meet Harvey Arden."

"How you doin', Hardy?"

We shook hands. He accepted a cold can of soda pop from our Eski, swigging at it slowly and gratefully. Sweat poured down his face, glistening in the silvery bristles of his short-cropped Lincolnesque beard.

"Got a new world for myself out here," he said. "Look at those mountains! Plenty 'roo and wallaby and goanna out there. Good tucker! And plenty good water at the spring down the hill. Everything a bloke could want."

"Had any rain up here lately?" Mike asked.

"Hardly at all this Wet. Bad year it's been. We need it bad, but I'm hopin' it'll wait till after the construction mob gets up here later this month. They're bringin' up a house . . . a three-room house. Gonna put it right over there. If it rains before they come, all my tools'll go to rust."

"This new block here part of your people's country?" I asked him.

He shook his head.

"Naw, not really. This was Ngarinyin country, not Miriwoong. But it's what they give me.... I'm happy to have it, get outa town.... Bring the old folks up to live out here. And the kids, too. Town's no place for 'm. All that drinkin' goin' on, all that humbug. Out here it's quiet and peaceful. No bloody grog out here. I won't allow it."

"How'd you decide on this particular piece o' land, Jim?" asked Mike.

"Well, you know . . . this here outstation movement . . . all Aboriginal people are gettin' a chance for a little block o' land o' their own. So I come up here, up Lake Argyle way lookin' for a nice spot. I picked Thompson Springs first. You know that water hole? Beautiful place it is.

"But the elders, they wouldn't let me build there. They use that place for tribal business. That's the Dream Ground for the eagle hawk. Eagle Hawk Dreaming, you know? An Aboriginal Dream site, a sacred place. So I had to shift from there and look for another place.

"So they said, why don't you come up to Dingo Springs with all them other people? Good people they are, too. But I wanted to be independent, start a block o' my own. A place I can grow me own family up. I got thirty-five, thirty-six grandkids, you know? They need a place to come . . . away from the grog and the humbug and the gamblin' . . . away from all that.

"I'm not goin' to live forever. If I ever die or me missus dies, then those kids got a home. Got a home for their whole life. They don't have to stay in town, they can just come out here and live a good life."

He waved a hand at the magnificent Dreamscape surrounding the bulldozed red-earth ground of his camp.

"Costs you nothin' to live out here, apart from bringin' up some tucker. You can't get a job in town. I tried and tried and tried. I tried at the hospital. . . . After I been workin' eight years as an orderly in a hospital, you'd think I could get a job there straight away. But I couldn't. No work. No work at all. I could go back drovin' on a station maybe, but I'm about sixty-three now . . . too old for all that kind o' life anymore.

"So, like I say, I kept lookin' all over for a block to build on, and I finally fixed on this place. . . . *Djunguin,* it's called. That means Alligator . . . Alligator Hole they call it. I'm on me own out here right now. I reckon by the end o' next week or so I'll have this shed almost finished. That's what I want, a bit o' shelter till they bring the house up. Once I get that finished, I'm right, mate. Miriwoong Construction from Waringarri'll build it. I'll be well organized by about January next year. We got about a hundred and fifty mango trees we'll be plantin' out here. Give us a bit o' fruit and some shade as well. We'll have a water system. Toilets. Solar power for heatin' . . . even a generator to back up the solar, 'cause it doesn't work all the time.

"We'll have six, seven houses up here in five years' time. Maybe twenty people'll live in the community here. Old people prefer bein' out here. It's good for old people. No place for them in town. They don't get drunk, most of the old people. They just sit there and watch the young people fight and drinkin' grog, you know? They try to tell 'm not to do it, but the youngfellas don't listen.

"The old people and the little children, too. They come out here, like it a lot better'n there in town. No swearin' and carryin' on out here. In town the little kids watch everythin', all the drinkin' and fightin'. It's no bloody good for 'm. When they grow up big they say, 'We can do it, too!'

"Me and me wife, we're goin' out to the airport this afternoon to pick up some of our grandkids comin' up from Karratha down south. They'll stay out here, go huntin' kangaroo, go huntin' goanna, go pickin' bush tucker. . . . Plenty room for 'm out here."

"How big's your block?" Mike asked.

Jim stood up and glanced at both horizons.

"Four mile this way and four mile that way. From those mountains over there to those over there. All that's ours."

HOW IT WAS BACK THEN

The conversation turned to the old days.

"Back then they used to *own* us! On the stations, I mean, before
we got tossed off. We were the property o' the station. We couldn't
leave. If you ran away, they'd follow you up and send the police to

JIM WARD AND FAMILY

get you and bring you right back. Police used to come up there and
give us a hidin'. Flogged us with a whip. Everybody—kids, grown-
ups, and all. If you didn't do your work, you got tied up to the tree
with a chain. No clothes on, they'd strip 'm all off. After the flog-
gin' they just left you there chained to the tree for a few days.
Figured that would teach you a lesson. Used to do it at all the stations, all the cattle stations. That's just the way it was.

"But at least we had work. We got work all the time. Today we can't get work. And they gave us bread and meat. We'd get coffee, tea, chewin' tobacco. Trousers and shirts got cleaned every three weeks. No money. No, not in them days. You got up 3:00 A.M. in the mornin' ... go all day ... maybe finish up at midnight. You don't get *no pay*. Nothin'! Next mornin' you got to get up again and do it all over.

"But at least you had a place to live, a place for you and your family. You didn't get chased off. In its own way it was a good life. I'd say a better life than the people get nowadays. Nowadays there's grog, there's gamblin'.... Some people get their pension and spend it on grog and gamblin' before groceries for the family.

"Oh, sure, we got pissed back then, gambled back then, too.... Today anybody with a car can go into town and buy a drink. Aboriginal people didn't have a car back then. Couldn't afford one 'cause they wasn't gettin' paid.... Coupla times a year the boss would tell us, 'Go on, you blokes, have a coupla weeks on the grog.' We'd come into town, have ourselves a bit of a drink-up. And after that they just come and pick us up in the lorry and take us back out to the station ... and back we went to work again. The drinkin' wasn't a constant thing like it is today.

"We used to gamble at the station, not for money but for shirts or shoes or blankets. Some blokes'd lose in a card game and wouldn't have any pants for a month! Nobody much minded back then.

"In them days the younger people used to watch over the old people. Now it's gone the other way round. Old folks have to help the youngfellas 'cause they're too pissed to help 'mselves. The old folks, no one looks after 'm now. That's why I'm makin' this place out here. Old folks can come here, and the kids, too ... get away from all the carryin' on.... Get back to the good ways, the old ways."

THE OLD LAW'S STILL HERE

"You have much to do with Law business out here?" Mike asked.

"Naw ... not me. Not really. Never really did. I been reared up with white people. My father was a white bloke. He come from England, ended up in the Territory. So I grew up there. . . . When he took off one day, I started livin' with my mother, with Aboriginal people. So I lived both white and black. Grew up till I got big and then started ringin' and drovin' on the stations over here. . . . Mainly Argyle Station.

"But the Law's still here. I reckon it's comin' back. The Law people, they still come through. Stops everythin'. People are scared. A woman can't travel on the road if the Law people are comin' up. Only men can go through. If they catch any woman on the road, well, they take 'm out in the bush and give 'm a hard time.

"Everybody respects the Law Men, even if they don't follow the Law. When the Law Men are comin' through, the old people hide the boys. Youngfellas get outa the way. They don't want to be caught by the Law Men. They know what happens. They don't want to go out there in the bush and be punished by the old people.

"The old men, they teach 'm to respect that old Law again. They teach 'm the hard way. When they do wrong the Law Men'll kill a kangaroo and cook it and then they'll throw the hot kangaroo over the boy's shoulders and make 'm walk, make 'm run maybe three-four hundred yards. Run all that way with the 'roo on their back and the boilin' hot juices runnin' down his body. It's a Law penalty. Then they pull the 'roo off his back. Leaves no mark at all, maybe a few bruises. But that boy, that bad youngfella, he'll remember next time he thinks o' doin' humbug. Won't do it again."

"You reckon it sorts 'm out then, the Law?" Mike asked.

"You bet it sorts 'm out, that Law. White man's law doesn't work. They don't respect it. They can beat it. But they know the way of the old Law. That stops 'm!

"The old Law, it's never goin' to die!"

DANNY WALLACE, NGARINYIN:

"I know this country. All through."

Fragments of a Dream

I COULD BARELY understand much of what Danny Wallace told me, and that, I suppose, was providential. There's something to be said for a lack of communication. Some things you're better off not knowing.

Here one of my "subjects" was finally telling me Dreamtime stories, and I could grasp only fragments of what he said. Even listening again and again to the tape of our conversation, I can make out only tantalizing snatches here and there.

Mike, whose ear has long been attuned to the wide variations in Aboriginal English, was having trouble himself. When I asked him what Danny had said, he would shake his head and turn his attention back to Danny's tumbling, rough-hewn words.

Several times I thought I heard Danny say "Wandjina"—but Mike insisted he never used the word.

"Nope, it's the name of some Dreamtime bird, I think. Tell you the truth, mate, I'm not sure myself."

So be it. Yet even in the snatches and free-floating phrases of Danny's speech, garbled though I've undoubtedly gotten them, I find a certain poignant meaning and essential poetry, and I will set them down here as best I can.

WHEN WE ARRIVED at Emu Creek, an Aboriginal settlement of perhaps a dozen small buildings, Danny was sitting on a blanket with several women and young children. Half a dozen dogs lolled docilely in the red dirt at their feet. Danny rose to greet us, a large, pear-shaped man with a pleasant face fringed by a short, white beard. Saying something about "men's business" to the women, he led us a few dozen yards across the compound to a

ribbon of shade beneath some gum trees, and there we stood in the fly-blown heat and talked.

I knew from Mike that Danny was a respected Law Man, well known as someone familiar with all the local sacred sites.

"Mining companies come to him to find out where the Dreaming sites are in this country. That way they can avoid offending the people around here. That right, Danny?"

"Oh yeah. Minin' blokes. They come to me. I know this country. All through. I use to walk around, you know? I know everywhere. We go out in helicopter. Find sacred place. I know all Dreamtime place here. I know where they are. Minin' blokes, they come ask me about that hill over there. That big hill."

He pointed toward a mountain in the distance.

"There a Dreamtime story about that hill, Danny?"

"Oh yeah. Dreamtime story about everywhere. I know the stories. Not mine but I know 'm. Old people tell me. They still travelin' there, you know."

"They?"

"Them old people, the ones who made the hills. Eagle hawk, you know. And white heron. They still travelin' there, makin' the country."

"Still? You mean . . . *now?*"

"Yeah. Minin' blokes, they lookin' for samples up there. Want me show 'm."

"What are they lookin' for?" I asked.

"Dunno. Might be diamond or somethin'."

"Don't they tell you?"

"No, no . . . they only samplin' anyway."

"You show 'm where all those sacred sites are?"

"Yeah."

"So that mountain is a sacred place?"

"Yeah. We people don' want 'm dig the place on sacred site. Keep 'm away from there. From Dreamtime, you know? From Dreamtime when they been travelin' before."

"Who's 'they'?"

"Him an eagle . . . eagle hawk. Him a rock sometime. White crane, you know? Eagle he get 'm a wallaby. Wallaby rock . . . in that place, inside."

"Which place?"

"Wallaby rock."

"Yeah?"

"Yeah. And kangaroo, too. He put a fire inside that white

crane. The rock wallaby did. And him come right on top of that hill. Right on top. Come out there."

"The rock wallaby?" Mike asked.

"No, the eagle. . . . Him have that thing, that bone, you know? He get that bone. Long time ago in early day. That hill there."

"So that's a special place, that hill?"

"Yeah. Special. Nobody touch on that place. Thompson Spring. You been see that place?"

"Yeah. I walked up there one time," Mike said.

"What's this he's sayin'?" I asked, utterly confused.

"He's sayin', I think, that there's this special place up there. Thompson Spring. Same place Jim Ward spoke of, where the Law Men wouldn't let him make his camp. And, what's that you say, Danny? . . . There was this eagle hawk, and he kept catchin' the rock wallabies?"

"Yeah . . . him just catch 'm rock wallaby."

"And what did the rock wallaby do?"

"Kill that kangaroo with their feet, you know?"

"Yeah? The wallaby did? Killed 'm just with their feet?"

"No, the bird. Eagle hawk married his sister."

"Who was this he was married to?"

"Sister of white crane. Him married eagle hawk."

"Say it again," I pleaded.

"So the sister of the white crane was married to the eagle hawk?" Mike asked him.

"Yeah. Two girl, both of 'm. That wife belong eagle hawk. The wallaby, you know? Eagle hawk him got long teeth. Eagle and white crane them argue. Him spear that two girl. Kill her with spear. White crane him say, 'Oh, you been kill my two sister. What for?' Anyhow, eagle hawk him eat the two sister belong white crane."

"And that's when he got that bone stuck in his throat?" Mike asked.

I was amazed he could follow the story well enough to ask a question.

Danny continued, gesticulating energetically as he spoke, waving his hands toward the distant mountain.

I knew I wasn't seeing what he was seeing. He was seeing into the Dreamtime, and I . . . I remained eyeless as ever.

For twenty minutes I continued gathering stray phrases.

". . . white crane him stick that thing down in the ground. And white crane him go sit down on that rock. Kangaroo, you know? Got bone stuck in his throat. Poke his eyes."

"Yeah?"

"Yeah! And him poke 'm in the heart. One time him turn into Wandjina."

"What's that?" I asked. "Did he say Wandjina?"

"Naw," Mike replied. "I don't think so. What's that he turned into, Danny?"

"Him turn into bird. Everythin' been turn into bird."

"What bird?"

"The old people. Him been turn into bird. Into eagle hawk, you know?"

"I see," said Mike.

"So them all still there, up on that hill. The old people, the birds. Them been turn into birds. All that Dreamtime. Them still travelin'. Always travelin' them old people from before."

DANNY SMILED AND nodded emphatically, satisfied at finally having gotten his meaning across.

Mike glanced over at me. I glanced back, one frustrated Awtha.

"What was that?" I asked.

"Haven't the vaguest, Harv."

No doubt Danny was having as much trouble grasping our meanings as we were having grasping his.

From the start, our conversation had been drifting in and out of the Dreamtime in phantasmagoric fashion. When Danny spoke of "old people travelin' " there seemed no way of knowing if he was speaking of old people of the community hereabouts, some Law Men coming through on "Law business," or some Dreamtime ancestors such as eagle hawk or white heron, which themselves took both human and animal form. For him, reality and Dreamtime were interchangeable, and you could travel back and forth between them as easily as walking between two rooms.

NOW THE CONVERSATION grew clearer.

"You born in this country, Danny?" I asked.

"I been here since little boy, you know? I was born in Northern Territory. Auvergne Station. Come down here while I was young boy. I been grow in this country."

"What's your people, Miriwoong?"

"Naw, not Miriwoong. Ngarinyin, that's my country."

"You ever go back there?"

"Yeah, go back all the time. Got all my brother up there."

"You have a Dreaming, Danny?"

"No, no . . . I don't know what my Dreamin'. My father . . . my father had Sugar Bag Dreamin', but I lost it when I left. It's back there in Ngarinyin country. Sugar Bag Dreamin'."

"Sugar bag . . . that's a kind o' honey in trees, Harv," Mike explained. "You get sugar bag around here, Danny?"

"Oh yeah. Plenty honey. Good stuff."

"Can you eat sugar bag if it's your Dreaming?" I asked.

Danny looked at me blankly.

"Sure. When I find it I eat it plenty. Not my Dreamin' anymore. I lost it, you know?"

"SO YOU SHOWIN' them minin' blokes the sacred sites tomorrow, huh?" Mike asked.

"Yeah."

"You go by helicopter?"

"Dunno. Might be."

"You been in a helicopter before?"

"Yeah. . . . But them fall down too quick. I been gone in that big diamond mine plane, too. Big mob! I show 'm sacred place. 'That mountain, that's blue tongue,' I tell 'm."

"Blue tongue?" I asked.

"Lizard. Blue tongue lizard. That mountain, that's Blue Tongue Dreamin'. Don't want 'm diggin' there."

"They find many diamonds, them mining blokes?" asked Mike.

"Yeah. Find plenty diamond. Lotta money in that."

"They give some money back to Aboriginal people?" I asked.

"Yeah. Give us money. But money no good!"

"No good?"

"Give plenty money. Buy us brand-new toilet everywhere, you know? But drunken people they smell 'm up! So money no good if we can't use them toilet, right?"

"Right."

I noticed a burly Aboriginal man with long, stringy gray hair walking toward us across the compound.

"Here come George Wallaby," Danny said. "Him proper dinkum Law Man, you know? Know more Dreamtime'n me. Lot more. . . . You been talk him now."

GEORGE WALLABY, WALMAJARRI, AND SON:

"I'm tellin' you this truth."

The Law Man of Emu Creek

7

DANNY SHOWED GREAT deference to George Wallaby, nodding at him without a word and backing away to leave us alone with the "proper dinkum Law Man." George, for his part, moved into the focus of our attention with ease and assurance.

"This here Awtha man, eh?" His powerful hand plunged at mine as if catching a small animal and pumped it vigorously. He carried with him an aura of confident authority. Half a dozen dogs followed him around at a distance of a few yards; only one thin-nosed yellow bitch seemed to lurk at his bare heels like a pale shadow, obviously the favorite. George continually shooshed at the others to keep their distance, which they did respectfully. He glanced about for a likely piece of ground, then led us over to it and sat down cross-legged on the dry, rust-colored earth, gesturing for us to do the same.

"Right here. Good spot," he said with a gruff but friendly voice. "I thank you for comin' listen to me. Always like a white-fella talk. We talk good, eh? You tell 'm what I say in your book. I'm tellin' you this truth."

"These your dogs, George?" Mike asked.

George had taken the yellow bitch into his lap, stroking her head affectionately as we talked. She gloried in it, purring catlike while the other dogs, pink tongues dangling, looked on enviously from afar.

"Three of 'm mine—that one there and that one." He pointed to two of the other dogs on the perimeter. As he lifted his arm, I noticed the horizontal tribal scars beneath his open shirt pull taut across his gray-haired chest. "And this one here," he said, scratching the ecstatically contented bitch behind the ears.

"This one here best goanna dog. Good fella for goanna, that dog."

"Yeah? You catch goanna with 'm, the dogs?" Mike asked.

"Oh sure. Find plenty goanna, them dogs. Find kangaroo. Sometime find emu. They feed me good, them dogs."

"How do they help?" I asked. "They bring 'm back from out in the bush?"

"Go huntin' with 'm," George said. "Go huntin' all mornin', all day, never get tired, them dogs. You know how we do it? We get goanna blood, kangaroo blood. . . . You show it to the dog. Rub 'm all over with that blood."

"You rub the blood all over the dogs?" Mike asked.

"Yeah. Rub 'm all over, them dogs. Then it'll be huntin' dog. . . . Chase goanna up in top of the tree. Then we can kill 'm with the stick. Sometime them dogs they dig goanna right outa their hole. Sometime he wanna eat the goanna right now, but he know we gotta keep the goanna for later, you know? So we give him some, give 'm just a part, because he kill that goanna and kangaroo. He have a feed. This one here best dog of all. Number-one dog. He know kangaroo talk. He know goanna talk. Can't see them goanna in the grass. Too high, you know? But he hear 'm talk, this dog, hear 'm go *khwanggg.*"

George gave out a squeaky, high-pitched sound that instantly alerted the gallery of dogs around us, prompting them to sit up and whine with sudden anticipation. The yellow bitch looked up lazily for an expectant moment, then curled back into the nest of George's lap and resumed purring to the loving strokes of his hand.

"Those goanna and kangaroo *talk*, you say, George?" Mike asked.

"Oh yeah. Them talk plenty," George avowed.

"What do they say?" I asked.

"Say watch 'm out you fella for them bloody dog!" George laughed.

He shooshed away a woolly brown cur that had braved an approach, flicking his fingers at it with disdain. The dog retreated, mournful eyed, returning to the others on the perimeter while jealously eyeing the pampered bitch in George's lap.

Now George's brow furrowed at some thought.

"Them doggers, whitefella blokes, they come here and shoot 'm in old days, them dogs. White man dogger. Dogcatcher, you know? Come in here and kill our dogs. Lotsa time they come. They say gimme money or I kill the dog. I say I got no money. So they take 'm. He ask me for this dog here. . . . I say, 'No, he's my life that dog. He feed us.' Still he gonna take 'm, so I go hide 'm out bush. That's how we save 'm. Make them doggers bloody mad! Like they wanna shoot *us*, too!"

"Why'd the doggers want to kill the dogs?" I asked.

"That's the white man way. He kill them dog. Shoot 'm. Take their ears off, then tail. . . . Go sell 'm somewhere. Back in old days we can't eat without that dog. White man, he know that. He kill 'm so we can't eat, that's what I think."

"YOU HAD MUCH rain around here lately, George?" Mike asked him, changing the subject.

"Not much. Too dry this Wet. No good." George scooped up a handful of powdery red earth and flung it at the dogs, who momentarily scattered.

"Get away, you dog! Man business we're talkin' here!"

He smiled and petted the bitch in his lap. I thought of asking him why the female dog could be with us for "man business" while the others couldn't—but thought better of it.

"You know why I think it is, there bein' no rain?" he went on. "There's no rain 'cause people been marryin' wrong these day. They don't wanna follow the old way, the right way. Marry the wrong skin."

Skin, I had learned, was the word for the ancient Aboriginal

GEORGE, HIS WIFE, SAMANTHA, AND SON TIMOTHY

kinship system—a web of intricate interrelationships dictating, among many other things, who can marry whom.

"So that's why it doesn't rain?" I asked.

"To my way o' thinkin' that's why," George replied. "In old days people married right, didn't marry the wrong skin. But them old days and old ways all gone now. And now the rains 've gone away with 'm. Everythin' wrong nowadays. Everythin' turn around, you know? Gone bad. People don't know who they are.

They got away from their own country, away from the old ways. Marry anybody. Marry crosswise, go against the skin. That's why the rain don't come no more. That's what I think."

OUR PRESENCE HAD attracted a group of children, who were setting up a racket nearby.

George glowered at them. "Go on, you kids. Get away! Can't talk business here!" He flung another handful of dirt, and they scampered off.

Now a young woman holding an infant to her breast cautiously approached.

"Damn 'm!" George muttered. "Hey, you woman you! You get outa here! Man to man we talkin' about business here!"

He flicked his fingers to shoo her away as he'd done with the dogs. But she stood her ground.

"Sick here, this child," she insisted. "Gotta take 'm doctor, George. You said we go. When you take us?"

George snorted. He looked at us apologetically.

"Sorry, mate. That's my promised wife. Samantha. That's my little boy she got there. He been throwin' up, you know? Gotta take 'm doctor."

"Can we give you a lift into town, George?" Mike asked.

"Yeah. Good on ya, mate. You give us a lift now to doctor and then you come back here tomorrow mornin', eh? We talk more business. I can tell you some things."

"Can we take some pictures of you and the child?" I asked.

"Oh sure, yeah. . . . But do it tomorrow. He sick now. And I"—he ran his fingers through his long, stringy hair—"I gotta fix up this hair, you know? Gotta look good for picture!"

We drove them into Kununurra and left them off at the clinic.

"Tomorrow . . . you come back here . . . you remember!" George called after us.

* * * * *

● ● ● ● ● ● ● ● ● ● ● ▼ ● ● ● ● ● ● ● ● ● ● ● ● ● ● ● ▼ ● ● ● ● ● ● ● ● ● ● ● ● ● ● ● ▼ ● ● ● ● ● ● ● ●

NEXT MORNING WE returned to Emu Creek. We saw Danny
Wallace sitting on the blanket with some women and children
again, but as we walked up to say hello, a burly, black-haired
man strode up, smiling wide with hand outstretched in greeting.

"Is that *you*, George?" Mike asked, peering at the man.

"Yup, it's me, mate. Who you think? I fix up hair, right? Look
plenty younger now. Younger'n you blokes!" He laughed.

It was George, all right. The long, stringy gray hair of yesterday

GEORGE AND HIS FAVORITE
GOANNA DOG:
*"This one here best dog of all.
Number-one dog."*

had been transformed into a slicked-down, lacquered black coiffure.

Danny, who had risen to greet us as we approached, now
waved a hand from afar and sat back down on the blanket, once
more deferring to George.

"How's your little boy, George?" I asked.

"Little fella him feelin' better today. Hey, you woman
Samantha, you bring that boy here now! These blokes takin' pictures! Put 'm in a bloody book!"

After the photo-op George brusquely dismissed Samantha and

the baby, shouted off the dogs, waved a warning finger at the encroaching mob of kids, and led us back to the spot of ground across the compound where we'd spoken the day before.

"Now more man business!" he announced, once more sitting cross-legged before us, Buddha-like.

"YOU FROM AROUND here?" Mike asked him.

"Naw. My people Walmajarri. Come from Billaluna, out in desert, you know? Long way away. Plenty far from here. I was born there. Different country that place. Got a big lake there and a little lake. And river, too. Lotsa water."

"That your Dreamin' back there?"

"Yeah. Floodwater Dreamin', that's my Dreamin'. . . . See, you look here."

With his index finger he drew a rectangle in the red dirt beside him. Inside the rectangle he drew a series of straight lines.

"You see . . . this Billaluna there. Floodwater Dreamin'. Big floodwater, right? When rain come, water it go bank to bank. And this one, this line here, that's Bush Fowl Dreamin'. And these two, this one and that one, those both Kangaroo Dreamin'. And here, this one's Eagle Dreamin'. And over here that's Crane Dreamin'. You know crane? Him look for fish, long-necked one. And that one, that's Devil Dreamin'."

"Devil?"

"Yeah. You know, Devil Man. Him Dreamtime fella. Devil Dreamin'. . . all them Dreamin's different tribes, belong different people. . . . Seven Dreamin's round there. . . . Seven different Laws. . . . If it's not my Dreamin', I don't go in there. . . . It's not my Law, you know? I can't go in there or there or there. Maybe I go in there. Maybe I ask their king and he allow me go through there."

"King?"

"Yeah. Big boss, big Law Man. . . . Gotta ask 'm. . . . So if he say it's all right you come in here, then I can go. . . . He allow me."

"So you were raised up in Billaluna?" Mike asked.

"Yeah. Live there till I was little boy. Then when I was growin' up, I was workin' in the stock camp. Argyle Station. Old blokes, white men, they been grow me up, teach me how to rope the calf, teach me how to work with horses, nail their shoes and all that. . . . Used to be white man land back there, but it's all blackfella land now. Aboriginal land."

"Those white blokes treat you pretty good in those days?"

"Sometime. Plenty hard work. They teach us, but sometime it's no good. We don't understand, you know?"

"Don't understand?"

"The whitefella way, I mean. They tell us how to do somethin', but back then we don't understand. Then they get mad at us. Like back then in those days we blackfella, we never use flour. We don't know how to use it. White bloke, he show us how to make damper . . . bread, you know? So they give 'm the flour, tell 'm to cook it. We never seen flour before. They say put it in the fire, so we put it in fire, that flour. Just toss it right in fire. *Poof*, it burn up! So he say, 'No! First you blokes gotta mix it with water until you make dough outa the flour, right?' So we mix water and make the dough, and then everybody start eatin' it just like that, without cookin' it again. 'Oh no!' he say. 'First you gotta cook that dough!' So finally we cook it up right, make the bread and then we eat it. Good stuff! So that's how we learn to do those things, them whitefella things."

"Life's a learnin' process for all of us, I guess," Mike said. "You learn our ways, we learn yours."

"Yeah. Sometime whitefella's way's the best, sometime black-fella's."

NOW A POLICE car came slowly nosing along the road leading into the Emu Creek compound.

George looked up, eyeing the intruding vehicle. "We got humbug here?" he asked, a worried look on his face. With a sweep of his hand, he erased the diagram on the ground, as if destroying some culpable piece of evidence.

The police car slowly drove through the compound, pausing briefly here and there.

"Coppers, them lookin' for someone," George said. "Always lookin'. Take 'm jail maybe. Maybe him run away from white man jail, you know? P'lice, they come and take a bloke and put 'm in jail, then he run away again. So they come lookin' for 'm. Sometime I tell 'm, 'Why you don't let us take care of 'm with blackfella's Law?' That way he don't 'cause trouble no more. We take 'm out bush . . . two month . . . three month. . . . Maybe even a year. That's our blackfella jail. Out in the bush. Better'n whitefella jail. Take 'm out bush and make a man of 'm. He can run away from whitefella Law, but he can't run away from blackfella Law!"

The police car stopped about twenty yards from where we were sitting. I could see an officer staring at the three of us. George shifted around, turning his back to them. He stopped talking and stared into the ground. I looked down at the ground myself, feeling an indefinable guilt.

"Guess they're not used to seein' too many white blokes out here, eh?" commented Mike.

"Mmmmm . . . ," George murmured.

The car started moving slowly again. George kept shifting to keep his back to it. The sense of menace was palpable. Finally, after several minutes, the car drove off, leaving the compound.

George looked up.

"They ever let you Law Men take care o' the troublemakers instead o' sendin 'm to white man's jail?" Mike asked, trying to restart the conversation.

George shrugged. He looked shaken.

"Good if we could. We sort 'm out if they let us. They never run away from there. Not from blackfella jail. If they run away we point that bone at 'm, you know? Kangaroo bone. Or special turkey bone. We point that bone at 'm and they get sick, those fella. They die."

"You don't chase them?" I asked.

"Don't have to chase. Just point the bone at 'm, that's all we do. Nothin' more. You can't do anythin' for him then, that fella. Pretty soon he get plenty sick. Go to white man's doctor and they can't find nothin' wrong with 'm. You can take him to doctor, give him medicine. But they can't do nothin'. Just get sicker and sicker till he die. He go, 'Ahhh . . . ahhhh.' He say, 'Come on, old friend, lift me up. I not feelin' no good!' But he got that bone in him now. No one can help 'm anymore."

"Really? No way to save 'm?"

"Only another Law Man can help him. But he won't. No way. It's true, mate. I not tellin' you lie. I tellin' you the truth."

"When you point the bone at him, how long before he dies?" Mike asked.

"All depend on the old people," George said. "Take two, three weeks, maybe one month, maybe two. He gonna die for sure. It's true what I tell you. That's blackfella Law."

He stared sullenly at the settling cloud of red dust where the police car had departed.

"Them come in here too much, them coppers. Too much! Always comin' in here. Lookin', lookin', lookin'. . . . Take our youngfella. Put 'm in their jail. Then they run away. White man law can't stop 'm. Blackfella Law work better."

George fell silent. He looked depressed. He scratched his finger aimlessly in the red dirt at his feet where the diagram had been. His eyes were lowered, avoiding ours.

Now he looked up at us. "You blokes . . . you tell them coppers to come here?" he asked.

"Naw, not us, George," Mike said.

"You sure, you blokes? You tell 'm come here?"

"Absolutely not, we'd never do that, George," Mike insisted.

"Mmmmm."

Silence.

Something had broken between us, at least temporarily. Further questions were obviously inappropriate.

"Well, maybe we'll stop back another time," I ventured.

George nodded glumly, staring at the ground again.

"Yeah. 'Nother time. Mebbe that better. I'm not feelin' so good right now, you know?"

"Well . . . I guess we'll be goin' then," Mike said.

"OK, you blokes."

" 'Bye, George."

" 'Bye."

As we drove off I looked back and saw George still sitting there, staring after us.

"You think he really thought that we . . ."

"Dunno, mate. Wouldn't blame him. Nothin' we can do about it, I'm afraid."

I felt sick myself, awash with an inner guilt.

Gadia's guilt.

REG BIRCH, "NATURE'S GENTLEMAN":
"I take these things very seriously."

Nature's Gentleman

8

NEXT MORNING WE headed to the local Kununurra office of ATSIC—the Aboriginal and Torres Strait Islander Commission, established in 1990 to administer federal funding for Australia's Aboriginal peoples and the closely related islanders of the Torres Strait off the northern tip of Queensland.

"I want you to meet one of nature's true gentlemen," Mike said.

We found Reg Birch, ATSIC commissioner for the Kimberley and Pilbara regions, standing at the reception desk with his wife, Margaret.

"A lovely and intelligent lady, the perfect diplomat's wife," Mike had told me. "Wherever you find Reg you'll usually find Marg hoverin' about in the background. Doesn't say much, but she's a power."

Reg greeted us with a warm handshake, introduced us briefly to his wife, then led us through a door into his office. Margaret remained outside, visible through a glass partition, chatting with Reg's secretary.

Mike had already spoken to Reg about the Awtha and what I was about, and had left a copy of *Wisdomkeepers* with him. He'd also filled me in a bit on the extraordinary man before us, among the most influential Aboriginals in northwest Australia, and one of twenty

ATSIC commissioners nationwide responsible for setting priorities and allocating monies for Aboriginal developmental projects.

"Used to run into him now and then in Wyndham when I was Wildlife and Fisheries officer there," Mike said. "He's a very special bloke . . . one of the finest ambassadors for his people you'll ever meet. He's got one foot in Aboriginal culture and the other in non-Aboriginal culture, and he treads the fine line between the two of 'm with the finesse of a ballet dancer!"

REG LED US into his office and slung his well-scuffed black brief-case onto the desk. The office might have been a schoolteacher's— plain wooden desk, a few cabinets, some chairs, a table, and that was it. Nothing flash, as the Aussie expression goes.

"Sit down, please, gentlemen." Reg waved a hand to the two chairs in front of the desk and sat down himself in the swivel chair behind it.

A handsome man, he reminded me vaguely of a middle-aged Omar Sharif, though without the arrogance of eye and manner. Rather, there was about him something simultaneously sandpaper tough and baby-powder gentle. An unassuming, almost sweet smile played continuously around the corners of his mouth, as if he were persistently amused by some unspoken inner understanding that we Gadia could not possibly share, but his eyes were steady and serious and probing.

He carried himself with a natural elegance, and I envisioned him somehow, despite his casual attire, in the gold-chandeliered corridors of international power, cornering presidents and kings and prime ministers and shaking his finger at them as he gave them a piece of his lucid Aboriginal mind. His voice, a soft tenor, was liltingly musical, and his language was as precise and as elegant as himself. I would have guessed he'd spent a semester or two at Oxford, but Mike had informed me he was entirely self-educated beyond the schooling he'd received as a lad at the Oombulgurri Anglican mission and Wyndham, his present home.

DON'T CALL ME A POLITICIAN

"You see," Reg began, fingering the collar of his crisply laundered white shirt, "I wear this white shirt. No tie usually, but a clean white shirt. My trousers are pressed. I get some flack from my own people for that. They think I'm putting on airs. They hate it when they see me pass by in a big flash motorcar or talking to a white person on the street. But it's something I have to do if I'm to keep in contact with the outside world. They say, 'Oh, he's just like a whitefella now. He's rich.' They don't know that the car's not mine or that I make a grand total of $423 a fortnight as ATSIC commissioner—hardly what you'd call a rich man's wage!

"So this white shirt," he said, again fingering the pressed collar, "it's a kind of uniform for me. A concession to being in public life. Frankly, I'd like nothing more than to chuck it and go bush!"

He laughed, eyes twinkling.

"I suppose being a politician requires sacrifices," I offered lamely.

Reg shook his head.

"I'd really rather you didn't call me a politician. I have a strong dislike for that word. I've spent my life *fighting* the politicians, you know. Oh, sure, I've been elected to this job, and they give me a fancy title—ATSIC commissioner for the Kimberley and Pilbara. But don't let the long title fool you. Really, I'm nobody important. The job's important, not the man. Call me an ambassador, if you like. But not a politician. I'm just a pair of eyes and a voice for my people. They've seen fit to elect me to this job, and when they vote me out I'll be only too glad to go. I have my painting and my writing and my music, enough to keep me very busy and very happy for many lifetimes."

"I SUPPOSE YOU'RE interested in writing about ATSIC, so let me explain briefly how it works. A bit complicated in its structure, I'm afraid, but I'll make it simple.

"I'm the commissioner for the state of Western Australia's

North Zone. That's the Kimberley and Pilbara regions—virtually half of Western Australia and one-sixth of the area of all Australia. There are twenty commissioners nationwide. Three are put up by the minister of Aboriginal Affairs. Seventeen are elected by the Aboriginal people of their own regions, and I'm one of those elected commissioners.

"What's important is that, for the first time in history, we control the total federal budget for Aboriginal affairs. We're also forming a state advisory Aboriginal council here in Western Australia—I'm deputy chair to that. We're hoping that will eventually lead to our having actual control of state monies for Aboriginals, too.

"So this is really a very exciting time in Aboriginal history. Hopefully, it will all work out, but it's all very new right now, and it'll take a few years to see how things go."

"Where do you think it's all leading?" I asked.

Reg took a deep breath, clasping his hands on the desktop and staring at us with a mercurial smile.

"May I be a bit visionary?"

"Go ahead."

"This ATSIC commission that we have now . . . it's my hope, my dream—and maybe you'll think I'm going troppo here, because there's already talk in some circles of killing ATSIC altogether, while it's still in its infancy—but it's my dream that it will be the forerunner of having Aboriginal people being elected *by* Aboriginal people to Parliament."

"You mean having all Aboriginals vote to elect a member to represent them in Parliament?"

"No, more than that. Much more. You see, we're not really one people, we Aboriginals. Aboriginal people from, say, New South Wales, are totally different from those here in the Kimberley. We're completely foreign to one another. Often we don't agree on anything or get along with each other at all. Just having one, two, or three Aboriginal members in Parliament will never do the job, I'm afraid.

"But *imagine* if, instead of electing seventeen regional commissioners to ATSIC, we Aboriginal peoples elected seventeen regional members to Parliament itself.... Each would represent his or her Aboriginal nation or closely related group of nations. Because that's what we are—nations! There are nations of Aboriginal people within this nation, and those nations should be represented in Parliament in exactly the same way there are representatives from each region within Australia. So *that's* my vision. Say I've gone troppo if you like!"

The smile continued flickering on Reg's lips, but his eyes were dead serious.

"And may I take my vision another step further still?"

"Go ahead, Reg."

"I want the world to see us, we Aboriginal people, as a full-fledged people among the peoples of the world. Someday..." He paused and wetted his lips, his eyes shining. "Someday ... maybe not in your time or mine but someday ... you'll see a seat established for Aboriginal people at the United Nations. That's my ultimate vision, an Aboriginal delegation to the UN, taking our rightful place among the peoples and nations of the world!"

Reg's vision hung momentarily in the air like a rainbowed soap bubble.

"SO YOU THINK real progress is being made, then?" I asked. "I mean, with the creation of ATSIC and all that."

Reg reclasped his hands atop the black briefcase on the desktop.

He shook his head, eyes momentarily downcast. "Frankly ... no. No, not really."

The rainbowed bubble popped almost audibly.

"Of course," he continued, "if you mean by progress that things are looking up a bit for Aboriginal people, well ... I suppose, yes. But real progress, if it's ever to take place, has to take place not among Aboriginal people but among white Australians.... There has to be progress in *their* way of thinking, in the way they look at and think about Aboriginal people. . . . And that's going to take a long educational process.

"Right now we're still really nobody in their eyes. We're nothing. . . . Until they really see us and hear us and understand the message we're trying to get across, really understand who we are and what we are and how much we have to contribute . . . until they stop blaming *us* for our condition and take a much harder look at themselves . . . well, I'm afraid real progress is still a long way off.

"You know, I often get criticized for saying things against white people. People say to me, 'Gee, Reg, you must really hate them!' But that's just not true at all. Hatred is the furthest thing from my mind. If we clash as individuals over different points of view, well, then, so be it, we clash. But that doesn't mean I'm antiwhite."

He eyed Mike with an amused expression. "You and I clashed a few times, didn't we, Mike? I mean, back in the old days in Wyndham, when I was trapping finches and you were a Wildlife and Fisheries officer?"

Mike squirmed a bit in his chair, obviously uncomfortable with the topic.

"Errr . . . clashed? Not that I recall, Reg. I was just doin' my job. Just keepin' track of what was goin' on."

I looked at the two of them, amused myself.

"Mike, I thought you told me Reg was an old friend," I joshed. "You never let on you were old enemies!"

"Enemies? Never! It was my job as warden to check people out, that's all."

"Isn't it illegal to trap birds?" I asked.

"Not back in those days it wasn't," Mike said.

A DANGEROUS LIFE

"So you were a bird trapper before you became a poli — before you went into public life?" I asked Reg.

"Oh, I've pretty much done it all at one time or another," he said. "I've worked as a professional bird trapper, as a crocodile hunter, as a fisherman. I ran my own bush tours and guided people around, like Mike here. I had my own shop at one time, even my own trucking business over in the Territory.

"When I was a young fellow I worked as a rigger in a pile-driving unit. All day I spent on top of this great big tower. Drove all the steel piles that built the Wyndham jetty years ago. If you made a mistake you fell. You know, it wasn't stationary, it was on a mobile pontoon, and it raked at an angle. You had to walk out on a plank and—*whoo*—nothing below you, you know. That'll get the adrenaline flowing! I was the only one who went through the whole nineteen months without ever getting hurt.

"As soon as the last pile went in, I left Wyndham. Got a job in Sydney. Worked there 1960 to '61. Darling Harbour, in the old marshaling yards . . . a pretty dull, boring job, actually. Paul Hogan—you know, the fellow who plays 'Crocodile' Dundee in those movies—he was painting the Sydney Harbour Bridge in those days, and I was down there below in the marshaling yards.

"I was also a deckhand on the pilot launch. I would go out and pick up oceangoing ships that came in from foreign countries. Meat ships, you know. You go out in the nighttime and drop the pilot off and, gee, it's pretty hair-raising stuff. Coming alongside these big ships way out in the ocean, out of sight of land, going through a big storm at sea, everything pitch black, waves breaking right over the top of the cabin.

"I *lived* for danger. Why not? I had no purpose in life. I never wore a life jacket. I'd hang on for dear life and say, 'Well, if I make one slip I'm gone . . . what's the difference anyway?'

"I finally got slowed down when I was twenty-three. Had this nasty accident. I was a shunter on the railway. The engine was behind us. We were shunting two big pallets of meat cartons on slings, and they just started to fly off everywhere. I had to get up and run, otherwise I'd have been cut to pieces. My foot went in between the railway tracks and got stuck. Train rolled right over it. I kept running and rolling and jumping. Couldn't figure out what was stopping me. Then I looked down and . . . *there was no foot!*

"It had come right off and was clinging to my ankle by the skin. It was still in the boot. All this bone was sticking out. This left foot. . . . Well, I looked at it and straightaway cut the trousers. Wrapped 'm around the ankle so the blood would run over it and congeal into the place where the foot was supposed to be. Then I unwound it and washed it all out, took all the broken bone tips and bound 'm together and then I just slid the whole thing back on, boot, foot, and all. Bound it all back together and *it stuck!* No time to pass out there, you know? You just do the bloody best you can."

He swung his left foot out from under the desk and wiggled it vigorously. The three of us stared at it for several moments with rapt admiration.

"How long before you walked on it?" I asked.

"Oh, about a year. I was thirteen and a half months in the hospital and a convalescent home. That was a hard time, too. The old guitar comes in handy at times like that. You think you're in a bad spot, but then you see all the others dying . . . cancer, stuff like that. I had a lot of time to talk to dying people. Lots of them died right in front of me. Had a room there filled with dying people. You'd smell death in the air. Pretty frightening experience, really. Gives you a new sort of perspective on life.

"Anyway, my foot was saved, though it had steel pins put in it all over the place. But that accident stopped the kind of rough work I'd been doing up to then. I just couldn't do it anymore. I ended up being very disabled. They offered me a pension then when I was twenty-three. I said, 'No, I don't want a pension. I don't want to go on the dole.' I don't believe in the dole . . . not for myself anyway. I figured I could always carve birds or paint pictures for a living, or go into some kind of business. My wife, Marg, has stuck by me through it all. That's the good thing. Without her I'd never have made it."

He glanced at Margaret through the glass partition. She had her back turned to us, deep in conversation with the secretary.

WORKING FOR THE PEOPLE

"So how did you get into public life?" I asked.

"Well, for the first time in my life I had to learn to use my hands and my head. I tried all those small businesses, like I said. It was quick and easy money, but I didn't really like any of those things. So I said to Marg one day—it was maybe twenty years ago—I said to her, 'Let's get out of it, let's get back into this other thing . . . this is the real issue, *working for the people.*' I knew it would be a lot of heartache and frustration, but it would maybe give my life some meaning and help other Aboriginal people as well.

"You've got to understand, up to that time I'd been just a wild man out in the street.

"Well, I thought about it, and I applied for a job in the Department of Aboriginal Affairs as a field officer. But when I got into government service, I realized that I really couldn't handle it. They were doing things that really went against the grain of Aboriginal thinking and culture. They were virtually digging our graves every day, and I got into all sorts of strife because I was constantly opposing the policy of the department, the policy of the country.

"So I took the first opportunity to get out of it, and I joined what they called the National Aboriginal Conference, which is a body put up by the federal government to advise the state and federal government on Aboriginal affairs. I got elected for the east Kimberley and spent four years there. That got me involved in international travel, and later I was elected the executive member for the Pacific region on the World Council of Indigenous Peoples."

"So you went from wild man to international diplomat," I said. "Quite a transformation."

"Transformation is essential for all of us, that's what I've learned," Reg said. "To change the world we have to change ourselves."

He leaned forward and speared me with his eyes. "You must *become* the change you want to see in the world."

THE CHURCH AND ME

"I was raised Anglican at Oombulgurri Mission," he went on. "A very strong church. Very strict. My mother and father were both into that. Not much choice, really. Lots of the old people still cling to it. But when I left Oombulgurri for Wyndham as a young lad, I got away from that white man's religion. I didn't want it and didn't miss it.

"Then, years later, I got caught up with religion again because my wife was what is commonly called a 'Christian,' and she probably saved me from a life of crime. So I found myself going to church again.

"My wife belonged to another sort of church, what they call a People's Church, a nondenominational-type thing. We were there a number of years. I even became church secretary. But after a while I could feel that something wasn't quite right. Something stronger was calling out to me. When church was finished on Sunday, the kids and I would rush home, take off those good clothes, toss on an old pair of shorts, and head out bush to hunt goanna or whatever. Next Sunday the kids'd say, 'Do we have to go to Sunday school?' And we'd say, 'Oh, yes, you have to do it.' But then we started asking ourselves, 'Why the heck do we have to do this? Because we're really getting nothing out of it!'

"I started asking people within the church, 'Shouldn't we be doing something more than this? Couldn't we do something to help Aboriginal people?' They said, 'Aren't you happy here? Haven't you got everything you want?' I said, 'Yes, I've got a car, a home, a good job. But it's not what I *want*. There's something else. I want to help my people be *somebody* in this world. But how can I do that when I'm part of something that's killing us as Aboriginal people?'

"I really started getting mad about it. I was jumping up and down about those things. So they told me straightaway, 'Well, you don't belong in this church!' And they kicked me out. Well, let me tell you, I never felt so good in all my life as I did that day when my wife and I just walked out of there. Ahhh, it was a fantastic feeling! And my wife—the one who got me into that church in the first place—she was the most relieved person of all! She stood beside me

and she said, 'Gee, that's the best thing we've ever done in our life!'

"So we knew we had to go out and do something else, something real, not phony. Something truly spiritual. And that something was Aboriginal land rights. Now, if there are people who want to classify land rights as 'political,' that's up to them. But to me, land rights is religious, it's spiritual, not political. To us the land is a spiritual thing, not political, not economic. Without it we have no religion, no spiritual life as a people.

"Political is a European-type term. Just like *sovereignty* is a Euro-pean term. We never had a sovereign, we Aboriginal people. Sover-eignty is a divine right. But we Aboriginals can only have that divine right over our own land, our own piece of country. So sover-eignty isn't really an issue. The real issue is rights to land. Not 'claims' to the land, like the government likes to phrase it. We aren't claiming the land. It's ours by right, by history, by blood, so we don't have to claim it. What we want is the right to go back to and have control over our own ancestral land, the only land where we can live in proper relationship to the earth, and to the Universe."

WE ARRANGED TO meet Reg the following morning at his home in Wyndham, a hundred kilometers from Kununurra. "I'm a different fellow at home, you'll see. I have my painting and my music and my writing. I can even get away to go goanna hunting with my grandson. I'm carving him a hunting stick right now."

Mike and I rose to go.

"But just one thing more," Reg said. "Before you fellows go there's something here I'd like you to see."

He unzipped the top of his black briefcase and reached in his hand to search for something inside.

Almost surreptitiously he glanced back through the glass parti-tion to see if Marg was watching. She wasn't.

His hand had obviously found whatever it was he was looking for, but for a moment he still hesitated pulling it out.

"It's something that I take with me wherever I go," he said. "It's a . . . a . . . *thing*, you know. A . . . we can't use the name. I suppose you'll think it's a bit *weird*. And, please, no photographs."

Again he glanced back through the glass partition to see if his wife and secretary might be looking, but they were still huddled in conversation, backs turned toward us.

"You know," he said, hand still inside the case, "there's a funny story about this old briefcase. Got pinched in London this past

September. Thankfully I got it back. Whoever stole it found that there was no money inside and they just discarded it in an alleyway near the hotel where we were staying. Somebody spotted it, figured it was an IRA bomb or something, and reported it to the police. So the coppers came with all their dogs and bomb-sniffing gadgets and everything. Quite a to-do over it! Anyway, I finally got it back. Good thing, too, because there was something inside much more powerful than any bomb!"

Delicately, as if it were a living thing, he extracted a small, thin, polished wooden board with spiral designs on it. It looked very old. He cupped it gently in the palm of his hand and held it out toward us.

I reached out to take it and hold it in my hand, but he pulled it cautiously back.

"This was given to me by an old man, one of the elders of the traditional people. It's a very sacred object. It's a man's object, and it has great power.

"The traditional people gave it to me only after a lot of thought. I didn't ask for it. I didn't know it was going to happen until the old man called me and told me, 'They want you to have this.' They gave it to me with the instruction that I was to carry it with me at all times, and I *do!* Right here in this briefcase. You can call it a good-luck charm, if you like, but, really, it's much more than that. It has power—real power—and it also has symbolism. It's alive, you know. I can feel its energy. Keeps me in my place whenever I get too high and mighty. Whenever my thoughts go off in the wrong direction, it reminds me who I am and where I come from.

"It never lets me forget."

As if having overexposed the sacred board to too much light, he slipped it carefully back into the briefcase and rezipped the top.

"I take these things very seriously, you know. *Very* seriously."

CHILDREN OF THE DREAMTIME

The Dreamtime Is Now

SEATED ON THE veranda of his modest home on a hilly slope above Wyndham, Reg Birch looked out on the Universe, eyes focused on the Dreamtime.

Behind him on the corrugated-iron outer wall of the house a realistic picture of an Aboriginal woman peeking out from behind some curtains in a window had been skillfully painted. From a distance, as we came up the road, it appeared that someone was standing there at the window.

Reg smiled and explained: "I used to have an entire doorway painted there, right on the front wall of the house, an open door with a man standing in it, looking out. A picture of myself, actually. From down there on the highway, it looks real. Keeps kids and strangers from coming up here and poking about when I'm not home, you know. Every so often I repaint the picture, just to keep 'm guessing."

Reg seemed a different person out here away from the pallid confines of his commissioner's office in Kununurra. A subtle transformation had been worked. He seemed physically larger somehow, more at ease and casual, and certainly happier, even serene.

A rough gray work shirt and battered trousers had replaced the neatly pressed public servant's "uniform" of yesterday. And his feet were blissfully bare. In his lap he lovingly held a guitar, strumming it absently while jotting with a pencil on a legal-size pad of paper on the round white plastic table before him.

"Composing a song, Reg?" Mike inquired as we walked up.

"No, no . . . just trying to remember the words of a song I wrote a few years back. I tried to sing it last night, and I realized I've forgotten a few of the lines. So I'm writing it all down."

He strummed a few chords, cocking his head and squinting one eye at the sky while silently moving his lips, then jotted down a few more words on the paper pad.

"It's coming back to me," he said. "Just takes a bit of remembering after all these years."

"Pretty chords you're playing there. What's the song, Reg?"

"Oh, just something I wrote for a local competition they had a few years back. It was a song competition about the Ord River, and all the entries were supposed to be titled 'Song of the Ord.' Their real purpose was to celebrate the river, how beautiful it is and all that. Kind of a promotional stunt for the tourists, you know? But I wanted to write down what the real issue of the Ord was—at least as I see it—which is how we've all but destroyed it. So I titled mine 'The *True* Song of the Ord.' "

"Could you sing a few bars, Reg?"

"I have a terrible voice," he said apologetically, putting his fingers up to his neck. "Hurt my throat while I was out hunting crocs years ago. I was chasing one at night through the mangroves when it suddenly came up at me out of the swamp and I jumped out of the way and hit a sharp branch. Bloody thing speared right into my neck."

"I suppose you lost the croc." Mike nodded.

"Actually, no. It was pretty funny, really. I yanked away, pulled the point of the branch out of my neck, and fell down right on top of the poor croc. Knocked the wind out of him. So I grabbed hold of him—no worries, you know?—and tied him up right there!"

"Mmmmm."

"That's what the song's about?" I asked.

Reg gave me a patient smile.

"No. Like I said, it's about the Ord. 'The True Song of the Ord.' Here, I'll play a few chords for you, but I want to apologize in advance for my singing."

He needn't have. His voice was a rough-silk tenor, highly pleasing to the ear. He hit a broad chord on the guitar, then coaxed out a lilting folk rhythm.

> *What have they done to our river,*
> *Dear bringer of life on the land?*
> *Once so majestic and awesome,*
> *Now choked, congested, and shamed.*

He sang several choruses, fingers blurring on the strings to a moving finale:

> *We should be condemned and buried*
> *For tampering with God's own earth. . . .*
> *Give us a chance to redeem you.*
> *You are not beyond rebirth.*

A last lovely chord shivered on the air, then silence.

Reg looked embarrassed.

Mike and I applauded, genuinely impressed.

"Really, Reg, that's terrific! So did you win the competition?"

"Oh, no. Of course not. It's hardly the kind of song to lure tourists here, you know!"

OUR RELIGION IS HAPPENING NOW

He laid the guitar flat in his lap, idly strumming the strings as he spoke.

"I was reading your book," he said. "There's a line by an old

Indian chief I especially like in there, about how white man's religion celebrates something that happened 2,000 years ago and to him nothing's happened since then, but how Indian's religion celebrates what's happening now.

"That's how it is with us Aboriginal people, too. And it's not just religion I'm talking about, you know. When I'm in white man's world, there in my office in Kununurra or wherever, I'm always thinking about what I said to such and such a government minister last month and who I have to meet next week, or what I or you or somebody else did or didn't do yesterday and what I've got to do tomorrow or next month. I don't have any time to think about *now*, no time to be present to the actual moment, you know? White man forgets the *now*, don't you think? We Aboriginals—and Indians, of course—we live in that *now*. To us, the most sacred time of all is *now*. Thinking about tomorrow or next year is a bother, a waste of time, really. But because of my position as commissioner, I've got to deal in white man's tomorrows and yesterdays while still not forgetting the Aboriginal's *now*. I've got to keep my foot in both worlds, you see.

"Anyway, it's just a thought I had after reading your book. So right now, you see, I'm just sitting out here on my veranda and enjoying the *now*." He gave the guitar strings a strum for emphasis.

"Of course," I said, seeing a contradiction here, feeling the need to come to the defense of my past-and-future-oriented race, "Aboriginal people *do* spend a lot of time looking back at the Dreamtime."

"Oh, no," Reg said. "No, we don't! Never did! We never looked *back* at it. The Dreamtime, I mean. It's *now*, you know? It's not some other time. It's *here* and *now* going on all around us. The Dreamtime never stopped!"

He strummed the guitar again, and for several moments the notes of a mystic chord stretched languidly on the air.

NOW IS THE MOST SACRED TIME

"That's why I love getting away and coming home here to Wyndham," he said. "Here I can forget about yesterday and tomorrow, just immerse myself in the present moment. If I have a memory, it's a memory I dredge up and bring into the *now*. If I envision tomorrow, it's a vision I have *now*! You understand?"

He eyed me doubtfully.

"Even sitting here talking with you fellows," he went on, "that's happening *now*, so I'm totally absorbed in it. Right here, this conversation, it's the most important conversation in the world because it's happening *here* and *now!*"

Was I getting a glimpse of an accessible philosophy here? Something I could actually use to hone the dulled edges of my own soul? To learn to celebrate the present moment, the *nowness* and *hereness* of life? *Now*, the most sacred, the most precious moment of all.

If there's to be beauty and wisdom and poetry, Reg was making me understand, it has to be appreciated, can *only* be appreciated *now* and *here*.

Trouble was, the thought was already a memory fading into yesterday. Even as I considered it, contemplating its abstract beauty in my Gadia way, the *now* was escaping me.

I wrenched myself back to the present moment.

WARRIU DREAMING

Reg looked up at the mountains in the near distance. They seemed to be pulsating in the rising heat waves.

"You see those hills out there? A magnificent view, don't you think? I can sit here in my chair on this veranda and look over the marsh and the water and up into those beautiful hills there and the mountains beyond. To me they're all significant. And they all have Aboriginal names, you know. I know each one of them, every creek and cranny and cave. We used to hunt up there as boys, my brothers and me. You know, I may not have much in a material way. Money is superfluous to me. Material wealth means nothing, it's pointless. But when you can sit on your own veranda and look out and see those hills and mountains . . . well, that's my kind of riches. I'll put a high price on that.

"You can look right across in the Wet season. It's like a big shining lake out there at the foot of the mountains. That mountain behind us in the Cockburn Range there is called Darraru. I've named my little block here after it. And that hill back there is Warrior Dreaming. In fact, this whole place around Wyndham here is called Warrior Dreaming."

Puzzled, I interrupted him.

"I thought I read somewhere," I said, "that Aboriginals had no word for warrior."

Reg squinted an eye at me, then nodded.

"No . . . that's true, but—I'm sorry but I think you've misheard me. I wasn't saying 'warrior.' I was saying *'War-ee-oooh.'* That's spelled W-a-r-r-i-u. This place here, around Wyndham, it's called Warriu Dreaming. Nothing to do with 'warrior.'"

"Oh. My mistake."

I wondered what else I'd been misinterpreting. No doubt plenty. If I could make so elementary a mistake even when hearing Reg's precise English, what other misunderstandings, from minuscule to monumental, had I garnered in recent days and months on this journey . . . or during my entire lifetime, for that matter?

"Anyway," Reg went on, "that hill—they also call it the Bastion, or Five Rivers Lookout—it gives its name to this whole area. That's why the official Aboriginal name for Wyndham is Warriu. It wasn't a place for Aboriginal people to live in the old days. It was a hunting ground, a Dreaming place where people came together. The tribes would meet here periodically to have their ceremonies and to discuss important matters."

"But it didn't belong to one tribe?" I asked.

"Oh, yes . . . it did. That is, this area right here belonged to one family, a family within the tribe. The whole tribe, meaning all the people who spoke that same language, had a territory covering probably several hundred square kilometers. And different families controlled different areas within that tribal territory."

"And what's the language they spoke?"

"There's some dispute about that. Anthropologists tell us this

was Worrora territory. But what we're told by the elders is that this was the territory of another people you don't read about in books, the Dadaway people, who spoke the Dadaway language. You don't see that in references at all. I think it's totally forgotten now.

"But they were the dominant tribe of this region around here. Wyndham—or Warriu Dreaming—was on the edges of their country. The center, the spiritual center, was over where Oombulgurri is now. But, to traditional Aboriginal people, the Dadaway are still the bosses of this country. There's no dispute about that, none at all. Even though they're one of the most forgotten, mis-used, and abused tribes, they're still the bosses of this land!

"You may be chased off the land and murdered, but that doesn't mean you aren't still the rightful owners of that land, that particular piece of land."

"So," I asked, "the Dadaway or their descendants still have a land claim on this area?"

"Like I said yesterday, we don't speak of land *claims*. Ours is more than a claim. We speak of land *rights!* Or, even better, of *rights to the land*. But the Dadaway people were scattered. Many of their descendants don't know where they came from, or even that they're Dadaway! Other peoples were brought in here from else-where for the mission and the stations. And of those only a few elders are left today who can remember how it used to be before.

"Then twenty years ago or so, after the mission closed and the stations got rid of their Aboriginal hands, the people just drifted to towns like Wyndham. They became fringe-dwellers. They were virtually penned in like animals. Several hundred were herded into a long building no wider than this house. Others lived in the rocks above town. They just lived and died there in pure squalor.

"Those of us who had come here earlier were the lucky ones. We had to help the ones who came later."

COCKROACH HILL

"You were brought up at Oombulgurri, Reg?"

"Only as a small boy. My family moved from Oombulgurri to Wyndham around 1944. I was about four years old. That was when the Japanese bombed Wyndham during the war. Everybody expected the Japanese to come in and invade. So the missionaries at Oombulgurri said, 'OK, all the white people have to leave and go down to Perth.' Ships came in to take them away.

ROAD TO THE DREAMTIME

© Mike Osborn

WANDJINA

© Mike Osborn

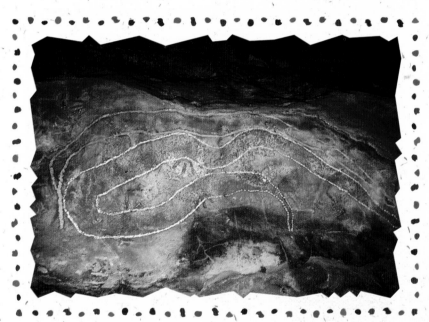

RAINBOW SNAKE

© Mike Osborn

THE KIMBERLEY: BOAB COUNTRY

© Mike Osborn

JACK JOHNSON: EYES ON THE DREAMTIME

© Mike Osborn

GEORGE WALLABY:

"That's my country…
Floodwater Dreamin'…"

REG BIRCH:

"The Dreamtime is now!"

THOMAS GALOVA PICKING

PITURI AT YAGGA YAGGA

© Mike Osborn

THE BALGO HILLS: EVENING RAINSTORM

(TOP) AND THE MORNING AFTER

© Mike Osborn

LEFT:

"I'm just a man, that's who I am!"

THIS DREAMTIMER ANNOUNCED

© Mike Osborn

RIGHT:

HEALER BETTY JOHNSON DOTES ON DAUGHTER VICKI AND

GRANDDAUGHTER ASHLEY

OUTBACK GOLD

JACK ROGERS "PAINTIN' UP"

TOP:

RAY ROGERS AND FAMILY

© Mike Osborn

BOTTOM:

THE "MOB" FROM LEOPOLD DOWNS STATION

© Mike Osborn

DAVID MOWALJARLAI:

"I know who I am. I have my identity."

"This is my brand, my identity."

© Mike Osborn

A SMILE AS BIG AS THE DREAMTIME

© Mike Osborn

The full-blood Aboriginals like my grandmothers they told just to 'go bush' and look after themselves. And the part-Aboriginal people—that's us—we were dumped here in Wyndham to live out the war. That was the hardest thing—being taken away from our full-blood grandmothers out in the bush. We lost touch with that old culture.

"So we ended up in Wyndham, my family and me. We arrived two or three days after the bombing. Wyndham was still burning when we got here. We lived in a shack we made ourselves in the old gully, the slum area, a little place called Cockroach Hill. You can guess why it was called that. So that's where I grew up."

"What tribe did you come from?" I asked.

"My father was a Bunaba man, that's from the west Kimberley. Same tribe as Pigeon, the famous killer and outlaw, as he's branded in this country. He's a hero to us, if you can imagine. I'm from his tribe, the Bunaba people. My mother was Miriwoong, from over just east of here. I'm from both peoples. But neither of those peoples belong *here!* And the people who *did* belong here were mostly scattered someplace else. So, you see, we're really displaced peoples in our own country!"

GROWING UP WILD

"Anyway, hard as that life was, I grew young and fit and strong and very big, and I found out that if I hit anybody hard enough in the right place they'd fall down very quickly and not get up. You could say I became a wild man.

"I guess I got my toughness from my father. Strangely enough, pretty much like me, he had only one leg. He fell off a cliff when he was thirteen, cracked his leg down here below the knee, and gangrene set in. Nothing they could do but cut it off. No hospital around here in those days, you know. So he went through life without it. Because of that he had to learn to use his hands and head, same as me, and he got a good position, became probably the state's first Aboriginal teacher's aide. He also became a builder. Helped his people a great deal. Sometimes misfortune is a great blessing. Cyprian Birch, that was his name.

"But one leg or no, he was a tough old bloke. He didn't waste any time talking. I'm more long-winded than he was. Even with only one leg, he stood up to people out in the flat. In those days it wasn't just one or two hits and a kick and a boot. Two men just went there and put pay to it, and that was the end of the day. One came back, one didn't. That's the way it was fought many years ago. We don't do that anymore.

"Usually it was fought with traditional weapons, fighting sticks. Here, I'll show you."

He picked up a stick leaning against the wall. It was about four feet long, two inches thick.

"This'll give you an idea of what sort of wood they used to do their fighting with. This is ironwood. Here, feel the heft of it. Heavy and hard, isn't it? That's all I need to kill a goanna. That'll raise a fine welt on you. They used that same type of wood. But can you imagine one five or six feet long and a good *five* inches thick? Big as that post holding up the veranda roof there. And they stood up toe to toe and smashed one another. No shields or anything. They only used shields for spear fights. You just stood there and took it, smashing each other until one of you went down and didn't get up. People don't fight like that these days because it's so . . . so *final,* you know? But it was very effective!

"So I still have that in me. Someone'll come up to me and step over the line, and I'll knock him down, I'll kick him in the guts or whatever it takes. I'll hurt people. That's what they expect, and this is what I know. That's what my father was all about."

CAPTURING THE DREAMTIME

Reg showed us several of his canvases, Dreamtime scenes but painted in a realistic, "non-Aboriginal" manner. One depicted a white-bearded elder in the foreground, with an Aboriginal family making camp on a riverbank in the background. Another showed the same white-bearded figure standing far off with spears in a mystic landscape, with a disembodied Aboriginal face floating in the air above a cliff.

"I've promised not to tell the stories behind them. I can't copy the paintings in the caves or even paint in that style. That's not my right, any more than it's yours to write down Dreamtime stories. Only a designated traditional leader has the right to paint those things in the old style. I might be a leader of sorts, but I'm not a chief or bossman, as they call them. So I have to respect that.

"But what I do is go out and talk to the elders. I make it my business to sit down with them for a few hours, even a few days, whatever it takes. I listen to their Dreamtime tales and then, with their permission and supervision, I translate the images into the modern idiom, as I've done here.

"Once I leave public life, I plan to spend the rest of my life painting the old stories in a new way. I also do a lot of writing — short stories in the contemporary manner, you know — setting down all the vivid memories of my childhood and the old days. Maybe I can't portray them in the old way, but I can turn them into visions of my own.

"So with my painting and my writing and my music, you see, I'm looking forward to a very happy old age."

WANDJINA FIGURES ON A CAVE WALL IN THE KIMBERLEY

Rainstorm at Balgo Hills

10

WE WERE HEADING south into the rusted red depths of the Great Sandy Desert just beyond the Aboriginal community of Balgo, which is some 200 kilometers south of Halls Creek, which is 310 kilometers beyond Turkey Creek, which is 300 kilometers inland from Kununurra. Another 90 kilometers ahead of us lay the Aboriginal outstation of Yagga Yagga, our destination.

"Don't want to get bogged out here," Mike said, pushing his sunglasses down his nose and peering out through the dust-crusted windshield, streaked and spotted now with snaking beads of moisture.

On the far horizon, a spectacular-looking rainstorm was building darkly above the enormous, shimmering Balgo Hills basin, which—reminiscent of the Badlands region of South Dakota—drops off abruptly from a high plateau into an eroded nether-world of reddish black volcanolike cones floating in liquid space. They had the dreamy look of underwater seamounts.

"Bet *those* have a Dreamtime story about them," I said.

"You can be sure o' that, mate."

The sun had slid behind a mother-of-pearl mist, and we found ourselves of a sudden in another world, silvery, soft edged, numinous with expectation. The stark red landscape had dissolved into a Chinese water painting. Great puddles in the ruddy mire of the road mirrored the hazy white glare of the sky. We drove through the puddles and through the sky and back onto the road. The car spewed plumes of muddy red water on either side and fishtailed wildly as Mike revved the coughing motor.

"That storm's rushin' right down on us," he murmured. "Better stop somewhere along here and wait it out."

HE DROVE OFF road and parked the car on a stony flat thickly dotted with sharp-spiked clumps of spinifex. Grabbing his tripod and camera bag, he jumped out of the car.

"I'm gonna shoot the bloody storm," he announced.

"Here, take this rain jacket," I offered.

He snatched it from my hand and was gone into the rising maelstrom, leaving me alone in the car, window rolled down, raindrops pleasurably pelting my face as I gazed out with almost religious wonder at the shifting Dreamscape inventing and reinventing itself before me.

Except for the white noise of the rain, it was an oddly quiet storm, soothing and gentle, more beneficent than violent. No high winds. Only distant thunder and lightning. I could hear birds singing joyously from somewhere throughout the half-hour downpour.

Not twenty feet off, the high plateau gave way to pure space at the sharp edge of a red-rock cliff. Out beyond, the swooning depths of the Balgo basin were undergoing a continuous series of subtle transfigurations. Rain, shadow, cloud, and sunlight raced one another madly across the surreal topography.

Where moments before the basin's desert floor had been dull and unreflective, now it had broken into a gleaming sweat. Water seemed to be coming out of the ground as well as out of the sky.

Silvery pools formed everywhere, and it seemed like the whole basin would become an instant lake. Those two seamounts in the near distance reminded me of a young girl's perfect breasts, black and glistening, hiding almost teasingly behind diaphanous veils of fast-moving mist and cloud. Tiny waterfalls spouted off the cliff's edge into the luminescent void. The black skin of the basin's floor wriggled with silvery rivulets. The whole landscape was alive, heaving, ecstatic. It breathed.

I watched, mesmerized. Surely this was Reg Birch's *here* and *now* unfolding before me.

AND THEN, ABRUPTLY, the storm was gone. The sun was already down, the sky fading fast. Mike returned, drenched and smiling, tripod and camera bag wrapped in the plastic raincoat.

"No idea if I got anything, but, my God, it was beautiful!"

He stowed his equipment in back.

"Whaddaya say we swag out right here?" he asked. "I'll fix some tucker. Think you could go for some lamb stew? We can make it to Yagga Yagga in the morning."

Somehow he conjured up a small fire out of wet scrubwood while I cleared a sleeping space for our swags among the spinifex.

"Don't want to go sleepwalkin' out here," he cautioned. "That cliff's pretty close over there, and spinifex isn't the best thing for bare feet."

"I'll stay near," I vowed.

After dinner he set out two little folding lawn chairs and uncorked a bottle of excellent South Australian tawny port. We lounged in sybaritic luxury, watching the last pale color drain out of the fast-darkening sky. The moon had risen, just short of full. The stars blinked on as if someone had flipped a switch, and there, just above the horizon, was the Southern Cross, tilting on its eternal north-south axis, giving the lonely traveler a comforting sense of direction in that otherwise directionless universe.

Far off to the right, some distant lightning strokes played above Balgo, perhaps ten kilometers away. The town's blue lights sputtered dimly at the top of a rise. We'd passed through there quickly on the way out, stopping only to gas up. I'd been surprised to see several of the buildings surrounded, fortresslike, by Cyclone fences surmounted with spiral rings of gleaming razor wire.

"Been a bit o' trouble here from time to time," Mike had told me. "Locals got pissed, pinched a truckload o' grog, then attacked some of the white administrators, it seems. They're just takin' a few extra precautions these days."

Balgo, in fact, had a notorious reputation for disorder, although it had seemed calm enough as we'd driven through. Two years back, a group of Balgo residents, mostly elders, fed up with the long-term drinking and violence, had staked out a new community deeper in the Great Sandy Desert. They called it Yagga Yagga—meaning "Quiet quiet."

"Had a yarn on the phone yesterday with Nelson Skeehan, chairman out at Yagga Yagga," Mike said, sipping the last of his port. "I told him about the Awtha, and he said come on out, they'd be glad to talk to you. Said bring along some cots, but damned if I didn't forget."

"Cots?"

"You know, to keep you off the ground at night. Seems there's been a plague of death adders recently."

"Death adders?"

"Didn't want to worry you about it. No drama, really. We'll be OK."

"You say you forgot the cots?"

"Yup."

"Oh."

"Sleep on the roof of the car if you like."

"No, thanks. I'll take my chances."

• • • • •

A COLD WIND kept me shivering in my damp swag all night, and with the first light of morning the flies came out, incessant and vengeful.

"Skip bloody breakfast," I said. "Let's get the hell out of here."

"Righto, mate."

Flinging our gear into the car, we jumped inside to escape the torment of the flies and drove off into the Dreamtime landscape in our air-conditioned space capsule. Breakfast consisted of potato chips, soda pop, and a corroded-looking chocolate bar that had been too long in the dashboard compartment.

"Damn good," I said, munching away, famished.

"Mmmm," Mike concurred.

PICKING PITURI, OR BUSH TOBACCO:

"Bloody bad-tasting stuff"

The Spears of Yagga Yagga

11

THE LAW MEN were coming, bringing Retribution out of the hot heart of the continent to the Rainbow Snake's wayward children. Following the Tracks of the Ancestors through the oceanic emptiness of the Great Sandy Desert, their slow-moving caravan of battered cars and pickups dragged a gritty cloud of orange-red dust from the Northern Territory across the Western Australia border toward the sudden mountains of the Kimberley.

Women—Aboriginal women—knew better than to venture out in the vicinity when the Law Men were about their "men's business." Sure punishment awaited those who accidentally met the caravan on the road.

On our way out to Yagga Yagga, we had stopped by and spoken with elder Betty Johnston in Halls Creek.

"Us woman not s'posed to see 'm," she told us. "We stay home if we know they comin'. Don't take any chance. It's dangerous stuff, this Men Business. Serious stuff. Secret-sacred, you know? Not safe for woman. You meet them Law Men in the road, you get hurt if you woman. Even children, boy-children, they beat 'm if they come 'cross 'm. Don't matter you explain. They beat you, do bad things those Law Men. Mebbe kill you if they like. P'lice they find you in the ditch next day by the road. You lucky you be alive. You shoulda know better. You shoulda stay home."

"And white folks?" I asked her. "What if they meet white folks?"

"You mean like you two blokes? Why, they just pass you by. They don't see you."

"And if they meet a white *woman?*"

"Same thing. Nothin', that's what happen. Only blackfella woman worry. Whitefella woman, she got no worry. Won't touch her, the Law Men. That Law's not your Law. Those Law Men just don't see her, that Gadia lady."

THIS WAS THE Law Men's second dread appearance of the year. Three months before, in January, they had swooped out of the desert in the dead of night and snatched the young boys, eleven, twelve, fourteen, those without the wit or will to hide, spiriting them out bush to "make 'm men." For six weeks or more they were subjected to the rigors of the ancient traditional initiation rituals, including the circumcision ceremony, spilling their blood into the sacred land, giving it—some say—its ruddy hue. Older boys, in their late teens or early twenties, those who had already undergone the first initiation, were "cut" a second time, receiving their chest scars and submitting to the painful additional subincision on the underside of the glans penis, the true mark of manhood—popularly called "whistlecock."

Now, in April, at the end of the Wet, the Law Men were back, this time on their mission of Retribution. This Men's Business is forbidden to outsiders. Forbidden to wives, mothers, daughters, children. To all the uninitiated. For an initiate to speak of such matters to an outsider once meant certain death. Dragged off by a band of Law Men into the bush, he would receive no more pity than a goanna or a sea turtle. A nulla nulla to the back of the head, splitting it like a spring melon. Half a dozen spears thrust through the chest, neck, stomach, groin. Left to the dingoes.

• •

But these were relatively benign Law Men coming. They were here to punish, not kill. Unless, of course, the need arose.

"THEY COMIN' HERE, them Law Men," Chairman Nelson Skeehan told us in the office at Yagga Yagga. "Carryin' the big Law. Comin' from Kintu over in the Territory. They be goin' to Billaluna, Balgo, Lake Gregory. Lotsa places. Come here to Yagga Yagga, too. Our own Law Men waitin' for 'm. Gonna get together and punish some fellas here at Yagga Yagga. Gonna spear 'm."

"What fellas?"

"Youngfellas who done wrong, you know?"

"What'd they do?"

"Humbug. Bad humbug. Some boys got a girl killed. Had a car wreck out on the Balgo road. Got pissed pretty bad. Smashed the bloody car and the girl got killed. Now the Law Men comin' to take care of 'm. It's the season. Gonna punish 'm, you know?"

"Maybe we're here at a bad time," I said.

"Won't come while you Gadia blokes're here," Nelson said.

"You mean the Law Men know we're here?"

"They know. They know. They'll wait till you blokes leave. Law business, you know. Gadia got no part in that."

"How many are comin'?" Mike asked.

"Plenty o' Law people all over the road. They call us here at Yagga Yagga this mornin'. Be here tomorrow. Boys are waitin' for 'm."

"Which boys?"

"Boys who done the humbug, the ones who gonna be speared. They waitin'. . . . That's one of 'm there." He gestured out the window of his small office toward a boy in his late teens lounging sullenly, hands in pockets, shoulders hunched, head down, leaning against a fence post.

"He doesn't run away?"

"To where he run? Nowhere to run. Sometime them boys get 'mselves locked up in white man's jail on purpose, but it's only worse when they get out. The Law Men, they gonna get 'm. If he run away, then they point the bone at 'm. The kangaroo bone, you know? Then he die for sure. Better take his spearin' and be over with it. Once he been speared, that's it. There's no more. It's over. So he's waitin'. He knows they're comin' for 'm."

"Think we could talk to him?" I asked.

Nelson shook his head. "Better not. He's plenty worried, poor bloke. Better leave 'm alone."

"OK if we hang around till tomorrow mornin'?" Mike asked.

"OK by me. Thomas here'll show you around."

THOMAS GALOVA, a slender, middle-aged man with a full, sweeping black beard streaked with gray, led us out into the beating heat and glare and flies of Yagga Yagga.

"You wanna see paintings? Plenty good paintings here. See, over there."

We walked over to one of the score or so houses that constitute Yagga Yagga and ducked gratefully out of the sun under its awninglike tin roof. Several women, surrounded by small children, lounging teenagers, and the usual lolling dogs, were sitting on the ground, daubing bright colors from an array of small bottles onto unframed canvases. They smiled at our approach, obviously delighted to see potential customers, and immediately stopped painting, gesturing at their work as vendors do.

"Nice stuff," Mike commented.

And it *was* nice work—quite striking, really. I felt a pinch of guilt. This down-at-heels Awtha had no intention of buying anything. They, of course, assumed that was why we were here. What else would bring two Gadia blokes all the way out to Yagga Yagga? Make a killing, you know. Get something at a steal. That's Gadia's way. Certainly not just to stop by, say hello, and have a yarn. Something about it rankled me.

"Dreamtime landscape?" I asked one of the women.

"Mmmm. That one there water hole, see? And there, them kangaroo. Goin' to a meetin'. Kangaroo man business, you know? Them meetin' at water hole for business. Gonna teach them young kangaroo boy all about big Law."

I saw neither kangaroos nor men, only bright floating dabs and blotches of primary color interlaced by wriggly black lines converging on a series of black and ocher circles.

"That the water hole," she said. "And them the kangaroo men. Dancin', see? Them dancin' around water hole."

"That water hole around here?" Mike asked.

"Oh, no. Not by here. This not my country. Water hole not out there. Water hole in here."

She tapped her temple, chuckling.

"You buy 'm?" she asked.

"Not buyin' today," I said apologetically. "Sorry."

"Mmmm." Her smile melted, and she returned to her painting, suddenly oblivious to our presence.

I asked her if I could take some photographs.

"Mmmm." She kept her attention down, away from me.

I snapped a few frames but then, nagged by increasing guilt, put the lens cap back on my camera. Damn, here I was stealing Dreamtime stories again! Wouldn't I ever learn?

A few feet away from us a teenage boy leaned on the wooden rail of the veranda. He'd been eyeing us with cool but intense interest, eating slice after slice of white bread on which he poured copious amounts of sweetened condensed milk from a red-labeled can. The viscous milk flowed off the edges of the bread, dribbling to the ground.

"Who you blokes?" he asked.

"Uh . . . my name's Mike and this here . . . this here bloke's an Awtha. Writin' a book, you know?"

"Yeah? Where is it?"

"The book?"

"Yeah, you got it?"

"No, I haven't written it yet."

"Mmmm."

He looked at me blankly, nodding contemptuously at the obvious charlatan before him.

With a snort he walked off, leaving a small white pool of condensed milk curdling among the imprints of his bare feet in the red dirt where he'd stood. The flies were already at it, buzzing contentedly.

"Nice breakfast," I remarked to Mike.

"Mmmm," he said.

This word *Mmmm*, I was finding, carried an infinite array of meanings.

"YOU BLOKES HAVE any tucker this mornin'?" Thomas asked. "Over there they cookin' somethin' up. You want some?"

"No. We're fine. Just fine."

I could feel the potato chips and corroded chocolate floating in the Diet Coke deep in my gut. Speaking of nice breakfasts. . . .

Thomas led us across the compound to a knot of people gathered around a pit fire on which was set a soot-encrusted kettle bubbling with something brown and wicked looking. I had a momentary vision of the witches' caldron in *Macbeth*.

Several empty boxes labeled "Fettucini" lay tossed on the ground around the fire pit. I stared into the kettle. Whatever was bubbling down there looked more like boiling red mud than soup.

"Mmmm," I said.

Perhaps twenty or thirty people were gathered around the fire—elderly men and women, teenagers and children, and the entire Yagga Yagga football team, a fierce-looking but friendly lot. I shook a flurry of hands. Several children were eating porridge with their fingers from plastic bowls, and one of these bowls was now thrust under my twitching nose.

"Eat!" someone said.

I looked down into a colorless mass of puttylike substance covered with a coating of sweetened condensed milk and raisined with living flies.

"Just ate!" I intoned, turning on my heel with a weak smile and looking for some escape from all this generosity. Just then I saw the boy, perhaps five years old. He was coming up to the group, face alight, his right hand outstretched triumphantly before him carrying the dangling body of a small goanna—perhaps fourteen inches long. It looked like it had seen better days. The boy kept squeezing it like a long toothpaste tube, forcing its guts out its lower orifice. A general cry of delight went up among the crowd, and the goanna, dripping guts and all, was quickly dispatched into the kettle. The viscous bubbles and swirling strands of fettucini immediately swallowed it.

"Ready soon! You wait!"

"Goanna fettucini," Mike remarked laconically.

Looking for an avenue of escape, I saw an elderly man out in the adjacent field with a couple of boomerangs.

"Hey, Mike! You ever thrown one o' those things?"

Making my move, I lurched out of the crowd and away from the dreaded kettle, pointing with sudden interest to the field and the man with the boomerangs.

Mike and Thomas followed after me, as did the footie team.

The man with the boomerangs cheerfully offered them to Mike and me. "You try throw 'm!" he said.

I took one of the boomerangs in my hand, feeling its heft.

"These come back in a circle?" I asked.

"Nope. Not comeback sticks," the man said. "Just for bird or goanna. Throwin' stick, that's all."

I gave mine as mighty a heave as I could muster, and it wobbled end over end in a ludicrous trajectory for ten or fifteen yards, landing ignominiously in the dust.

A roar of laughter went up from the watching crowd.

Now Mike, his face suddenly serious, stepped up to take his turn. With the grace of a discus thrower, he spun in a tight half circle and let fly with the boomerang. It whirred into the air like a helicopter's rotor blade and sailed a good forty yards or more.

Applause burst from the appreciative crowd.

"Not bad," I begrudged him.

"Want to try again?" he asked.

"No thanks," I demurred.

YOUNG HUNTER OF YAGGA YAGGA:

". . . His right hand outstretched triumphantly before him carrying the dangling body of a small goanna."

"Say, what's goin' on over there?" I asked, spotting a group of elderly men gathered together, chanting under the tin-roofed veranda of one of the houses just across the compound. The aluminum siding of one wall bore a painting of a large goanna surrounded by red and blue handprints—much like those I had seen in several rock-art sites.

"Oh, them Law Men," said Thomas. "Waitin' for the others, that big mob comin' from Kintu. They sharpenin' their punishment spears over the fire."

"Think we could have a yarn with 'm?" I asked.

Thomas cocked his head uncertainly. "I'll ask 'm," he said.

Mike and I stood a few yards off while Thomas ambled over and spoke with the men.

The chanting stopped. The men looked up at us, whispering conspiratorially among themselves. Finally Thomas walked back, nodding.

"I TOLD 'M YOU doin' a book. They say OK to come over and yarn awhile. But *no pictures*, they say. And *no tape recorder . . . and don't use their names* in your book!"

My Awtha's soul groaned within me.

Here was The Scene. Law Men in action, sharpening their punishment spears, preparing for the ancient ceremony of Retribution. I'd stumbled across the edges of the Dreamtime at last. But—no camera, no tape recorder, no names.

"Them pretty old, them blokes," Thomas said, attempting an explanation. "Mebbe them be gone soon. Die, you know? If people out here see their picture there in that book after that old bloke's gone, well . . . they get bloody upset. Not s'pose to see their picture. Not even s'pose to say their name or read their name."

"Why's that?" I asked.

"Make 'm come back, that bloke. Spirit, you know? Ghost. Come back and bother us."

Mike had told me earlier of this aversion to naming the deceased during the first year or two after their death—a prohibition still followed in the more traditional communities out here in the desert. On one of his previous trips to Yagga Yagga, some local men had visited Mike's camp, and he'd asked them if they wanted him to "boil up a billy" for tea.

"Well, seems an old bloke named Billy had just died. I'd violated the taboo against naming the recently dead. They clammed up, wouldn't look at me again the rest of the day. Took quite a while before they opened up again."

Now we strolled up to the Law Men, seven in all, gathered on the red-dirt floor beneath the cooling shade of the tin roof. Several squatted around two small fires, across which lay a half dozen slender blackened-wood spear shafts and blades. Others sprawled on the ground on hips and elbows, scraping and polishing the lengths of wood. They paid us little attention, talking among themselves in "language," apparently joking about something. Us most likely. All were barefoot and bare chested, wearing battered trousers or shorts—except for one elderly man, the only one standing, who wore a belted, priestlike white robe with a large bishop's cross hanging around his neck and had about him an important air. He quietly honed a spear shaft with a large file. I could feel his eyes on me. Later I asked Thomas who he was, but Thomas only shook his head and said blankly, "Just a bloke. Law bloke, you know."

I pressed no further. What I needed to be told I would be told.

Mike and I sat down on the ground in the Law Men's midst.

"So what you fellas doin'?" I blurted out stupidly.

Their laughter stopped. Seven pairs of eyes swiveled around and focused on me.

There was a momentary cold silence.

Finally the old gent with the bishop's cross held out the spear he'd been filing and pointed its blackened tip straight at me as if taking aim.

"Makin' spear. For punish them youngfella. In the leg, you know?"

He brandished the point in the air, circling it in the direction of my outstretched leg.

"Mebbe punish you, too!"

The Law Men all laughed. After an uncertain moment, so did I. The chill dissolved. But I asked no more questions, stupid or otherwise. I was content simply to be there, immersing myself in Reg Birch's *here* and *now*.

One slender old bloke was sprawled out beside me in the dirt, his head resting on a bent coffee tin for a pillow. I offered him a cigarette, which he took with a grateful smile. I passed him my plastic lighter, and this he fumbled with for several seconds, unable to strike a flame. I reached out to help him, but he shook his head and handed the lighter back to me. Snatching a small glowing brand from the fire, he lit the cig and puffed deeply.

For perhaps twenty minutes Mike and I sat there among them, saying little, grateful just to watch. The Law Men worked assiduously at their spears, chanting under their breath. They passed among them a large file, a small ax, and a handmade scraper consisting of a carved wooden handle with sharpened pieces of metal inserted as scrapers at either end. With these they worked the spear shafts and wooden blades—filing, whittling, honing. They joked in "language" among themselves, paying us no heed.

Finally one of the Law Men, a rotund fellow of perhaps seventy with prominent chest scars, rose and said something to Thomas, then walked off, carrying a couple of spears.

The man with the robe and large cross, I noticed, had also disappeared. Fearing they would all do the same, I sensed our welcome was over and got up to go.

"Thanks for lettin' us watch," I said.

"Mmmm," came the general response.

They didn't look up.

"What'd that bloke say to you?" I asked Thomas as we walked away.

"Says come on over, wants me to do 'm a favor, he says."

We walked over to another small fire about twenty yards off, where the rotund elder had now taken his seat to continue working on his spears alone.

He and Thomas spoke in "language" for a few moments, and Thomas nodded affirmatively at whatever it was he was saying.

I wondered whether he spoke English at all, but then he gestured with his hand for Mike and me to sit down.

"Have a seat, you blokes."

We sat down on the ground before him. He was rubbing a small spear, perhaps five feet long, with an oily rag. The other spear, perhaps seven feet long, lay on the ground at his side.

He held the smaller one in the air.

"This one for goanna," he said. "Woman's stick. And this one"—he picked up the longer spear—"this one for punishin' them youngfella."

He set down both spears and raised one of his legs slightly off the ground.

"See this?"

He pointed at some ugly dark scars on the meaty underside of one thigh.

"Law Men do that. Spear me in leg right here when I was youngfella. Spear go in right here, see? And come out right there!"

He laughed, rubbing his thigh as if it still hurt.

"They throw 'm at you, those spears?" Mike asked.

"Oh, no. Not throw 'm. Come up like this, see?"

He took the larger spear and set its point up against the scars on his underthigh.

"Don't throw 'm. They *push* . . . push 'm right in!"

He made a motion with his hand, as if pushing the spear tip forcefully through his thigh.

"That where you try and push 'm. Right there. That way them can walk again, you know? Spear 'm wrong way and can't walk. Gotta spear 'm careful. Don't wanna make 'm cripple. Them boys, they gotta be able walk."

He put down the spear.

"My son, my own boy," he said. "Got 'mself in bad trouble. There in Kununurra. P'lice, they arrest 'm. Take 'm to court. I go and tell 'm, that judge, I tell 'm, 'Don't put 'm in jail,' I say. 'You give 'm to us. You give 'm to us and we punish 'm plenty. Won't do humbug no more after that.'"

"And?" Mike asked.

"So they give 'm to us. We take 'm out bush. I take my spear." He picked up the long spear again and made a sharp jabbing motion with it. "I spear 'm," he said.

"You did yourself? Your own son?" I asked.

"Spear 'm right in leg I did. No more humbug. Him OK boy now!" He smiled with deep satisfaction.

I noticed that part of his left thumb was missing, and he had a large, nasty-looking scar seemingly out of place on one shoulder. He saw me looking it at.

"Got that in fight long time ago. Long long time. Cut me with big knife. Bad fella did."

He rubbed the scar with his fingers, momentarily lost in thought. Then, abruptly laughing, he looked me in the eye and announced, "But I cut that bloody bloke worse'n he cut me!" His face beamed.

"Good on ya!" Mike said.

The Law Man gave a contented grunt and began rubbing the small spear with the oily rag again.

He said not another word.

Thomas nodded at us. It was time to go. We'd been given all that could be given.

"WHAT'S THAT FAVOR he was askin' you?" I asked Thomas as we headed for the car.

"I tell 'm I'm takin' you blokes up the hill for a lookaround," Thomas said. "He ask me to find 'm some bush tobacco, if I see some. Maybe up in the cave, we'll see."

We drove a kilometer or so to a rugged brownstone scarp and climbed a few hundred feet among rough boulders to a rock overhang. Some badly faded paintings, barely recognizable as such, could be seen on the smoke-darkened ceiling. Thomas got down on his haunches, picking among some dry weeds growing in a small crevice.

"Rubbish. Too dry," he said. "No bloody good."

He searched farther along the inner edges of the overhang,

finally coming to several more plants that showed a touch of green.

"This not too bad," he said, rubbing the leaves between his fingers.

He pulled out a handful of the weeds, stared at them critically for a moment, then stuffed them into the pocket of his shorts.

"They get high on that stuff?" I asked Mike.

"That's what I'm told, mate. Pituri, they call it. Bush tobacco. Bloody bad-tastin' stuff."

"How they use that stuff?" I asked.

"Oh, crush it and chew it, you know. Gotta fix it special way."

"You don't smoke it?"

He shook his head. "Give you a bad head you smoke it."

"You mix it with ashes, don't you?" Mike asked.

Thomas nodded grudgingly, obviously getting uncomfortable with the subject.

"Special way. Gotta do it special way."

He would say no more.

THE THREE OF us sat on a rock ledge and looked out at the unreeling Dreamtime topography below us, a tremendous reddish brown, almost treeless flatland striated by long parallel lines fading off into distant haze. The lines, I knew, were actually thirty-foot-high red-sand dunes—the bane of early travelers—extending ruler-straight for hundreds of kilometers through the Great Sandy Desert.

"So that's Yagga Yagga down there?" I asked, pointing to two small water towers shimmering miragelike in the far distance.

"Yeah, that Yagga Yagga. Way down there. Look pretty small from up here," Thomas said. "But it plenty big place now. Big mob livin' there. Gettin' too big, I think. Used to be empty place here just a coupla year back. Dream place, you know?"

"Dream place?"

"Yeah, this hill here and that one over there, both hills. Made by two young men, twin blokes in the Dreamtime. Them two they been travelin' all over the place. Still out there somewhere, makin' hills, you know? Wherever they go, they make hills. They out huntin' snakes, those blokes. Come right here. Make these two hills. They dig, dig, dig for snakes. So they dig right here, make this cave right here diggin' for snakes."

"The Rainbow Snake?" I asked.

"Naw, just bloody snakes."

WE DROVE BACK to Yagga Yagga to drop Thomas off.

"Any suggestion where we could make camp?" Mike asked him.

BUSH POTATOES

He pointed to the two water towers at the compound's edge — the same water towers that had seemed so tiny from the cave.

"Good place there," he said.

"What's this Mike was tellin' me about death adders?" I ventured.

"True. Been lots of 'm around lately. Gotta watch 'm," Thomas said. "Better'n scorpion, though."

"Scorpions?"

"Yup. Them been plenty bad round here, too. But them bloody death adder eat the scorpion!"

"Anyone been bitten?" I asked.

"Little girl," he said. "She been playin' with one o' them scorpion. Kids, you know. Got good eyes at night. She see scorpion and pick 'm up to play with. Better not to see 'm. Then you're not scared! But no worry, mate. You let 'm alone you get along pretty good with 'm."

"Same for the death adders?"

"Mmmm."

"Don't have any extra cots around, do you?"

Thomas shook his head. "Nope. All bein' used."

I accepted my fate.

We parked the Toyota at the water towers and started to make camp perhaps twenty yards from the nearest houses. A flock of white cockatoos rose into the darkening sky from their platform atop the water towers and squawked raucously at our approach. From Yagga Yagga's compound came a welter of noises—dogs barking, children squealing, the generator humming, a truck repeatedly revving its consumptive motor. One woman cried out loudly time and again, I've no idea about what. Her shrill voice vied with the cockatoos. Now an old man, one of the Law Men we had seen earlier, came striding out between two houses shouting at some children who were dogging his heels, taunting him. He swung a boomerang wildly around his head, threatening his persecutors. Laughing hilariously, they darted just out of his reach.

"You say Yagga Yagga means 'Quiet quiet'?" I asked Mike.

"That's what they say, mate."

Trash lay strewn everywhere around our camp. Apparently, the spot was used as a convenient dump. The flies were ravenous, droning in clouds around our heads.

I had a sudden inspiration.

"What say we look for a spot out bush?"

"Flies just as bad out there, I'm afraid."

"Let's chance it."

Mike shrugged, tossed our gear back in the car, and we drove a few kilometers out, looking for a likely spot.

"What's that tent?" I asked, noticing a neat green tent perched alluringly among some low dunes.

"Some bloke's camp. Must be away."

We parked and found a tidy camp replete with stone fireplace, utensils, and stacks of tinned food all neatly in place as if the owner would be back momentarily. The tent itself was an airy thing, square shaped, made of green-tinted mosquito netting. I pulled aside the netting and ducked inside. Within I saw a foot-locker with the word "PRIVATE!" scrawled on it and . . . *two cots!*

"Looks lovely," I said. "I don't suppose . . ."

"Toss your swag in there." Mike said, "I'll fix some tucker."

"The owner won't mind?"

"Outback hospitality, mate. Be sure you pick up your cigarette butts."

"Which cot do you want?"

"Not me. I'll swag out by the fire. Cooler breeze out here. You take the tent."

I hauled my swag and gear inside, closed the weighted door flap against the flies, and sprawled out gratefully on one of the cots, wallowing in my newfound luxury. After several nights swagging on rocky ground, I couldn't have been more delighted. To hell with scorpions and death adders!

Nightfall brought a blessed end to the flies. And then the mosquitoes came up. The damn tent was filled with them!

"Try that spray on the shelf in there!" Mike called out.

I gassed the tent's interior thoroughly and staggered out, coughing.

"Bloody mozzies," Mike said. "Worse here'n Yagga Yagga. One thing doesn't get you, another will."

We ate dinner in agony, swatting our tormentors with futility.

They whined in my ears like tiny dentist drills.

"At least the flies are gone," I philosophized.

"They'll be back, mate."

God, I hated all this outback wisdom. Particularly when it was true.

NEXT MORNING THE flies again made breakfast impossible. We left a note of thanks and a few tins of tuna for the owner and scoured the campsite clean as we'd found it.

Driving back through Yagga Yagga, we saw no sign of the Law Men. The place looked nearly deserted.

"Where's everybody?" Mike asked an elderly woman.

"Gone to a footie game in Billaluna," she said.

We drove on through, slaloming among huge red puddles on the road back to Balgo. The site where we'd been visited by that silvery rainstorm over the Balgo Hills on the way out now seemed strangely quiescent, the landscape dull and unreflective again. Those two seamounts that had glistened like perfect black breasts two days earlier looked utterly unevocative today, two ordinary brown-red hills floating in a murky haze.

Strange how the Dreamtime comes and goes.

"Think we'll pass that caravan of Law Men along the road?" I asked Mike.

"Probably won't be comin' through till this afternoon from what Nelson tells me."

We were heading to Halls Creek to spend a few days with Jack and Betty Johnston, old friends of Mike's.

"Is Jack a Law Man?" I asked.

"Oh, no, not old Jack," Mike said. "He wasn't raised that way. Grew up on a station here around Halls Creek. Lived among white people. Coupla months back I stopped by to see him and Betty and he asked me if I could drive him out to his camp in the bush. This was in January, when all that Law business was goin' on, initiatin' the young men and all of that. He had to get some-thing from his camp for some reason, so I said I'd take him out there. Well, he laid down in the back of the car the whole way. From the time we left Halls Creek you couldn't see his head in the back of the car. We came by a car broken down in the road, saw a mob o' young blokes millin' around, and I slowed down to see if they needed a hand. But old Jack hissed out from the back-seat, 'Don't stop! Don't stop! Mebbe Law Men! Just keep goin'! Keep goin'!' He really got quite excited about it. Actually, they were just everyday blokes from Halls Creek, not Law Men, but Jack wasn't takin' any chances."

"I thought only women had to be afraid."

"Anyone who's not initiated is the way I understand it. Anyone Aboriginal, that is. Never any tellin' what the Law blokes might do . . . beat him up maybe, drag him off into the bush and make him go through some ceremony. Or maybe just ignore him. Hard to tell.

"These folks up at Halls Creek, as you'll see, don't all follow the Law, that's true, but they *believe* in it!"

WE DROVE THROUGH Balgo again, gassing up for the 300 k's of corrugated hell back to Halls Creek. Like Yagga Yagga, the town was nearly deserted. As we headed out, we saw a lone youth limping slowly across the central square, obviously in pain. Both of his thighs were wrapped in broad white bandages.

"Looks like the Law Men have been here!" Mike said.

Next day, after we checked into a blessedly modern motel in Halls Creek, Mike rang Nelson Skeehan back at Yagga Yagga to thank him for his hospitality. He asked Nelson if the Law Men had made their appearance yet.

"Oh, yeah," Nelson told him. "Came in the afternoon. Speared those young blokes in the leg! They're all plenty glad it's over. They want to heal up in time for the next footie season!"

HEALER BETTY JOHNSTON:
"You gotta buhLEEVE!"

The Healer's Touch

12

"LET ME PUT my arms around you!" healer Betty Johnston declared as Mike and I walked up to the concrete veranda of her little government-built cinderblock house in Halls Creek. She and I had hit it off during our brief visit on the way out to Yagga Yagga a few days before, and now we stood hugging each other like old friends in the sticky heat, mingling sweat and affection. Her body was warm and solid and strong, terribly real somehow, radiating a palpable physical energy that belied the nearly seventy years she wore so lightly.

"I'm a toucher," she said. "I got to hold someone to know 'm."

Touching her made me feel more real myself.

Her veranda—like all Aboriginal verandas—was the center of the Universe. Narrow and L-shaped, comprising no more than a couple closets worth of space, it provided the stage for an ever-changing concourse of humanity. Friends, neighbors, relatives continually flowed through as if something quite essential were to be found here and only here.

There sat old Jack, Betty's husband, the patriarch, hands over his paunch, half-sleeping, smiling benignly, children crawling on and off his copious lap. There was his daughter Sylvia, a pretty, full-bodied matron, gleaming with sweat and energy, talking a streak to any and all around her, shouting occasionally at the rollicking children without effect. There on the veranda step sat grandson Des, a handsome young fellow in his early twenties, deejay at the local Aboriginal radio station, avidly reading the copy of *Wisdomkeepers* I'd brought along. On a cot beside one wall sat robust Rebecca, another of Jack and Betty's daughters, and her white husband, Jock, a barrel-chested man who prospected with a bulldozer and metal detector out in the goldfields around Halls Creek. Beside him, Betty's lovely granddaughter Vicki nursed a diapered girl-baby with the widest brown eyes this side of the Dreamtime.

"That's Ashley, the baby there. My great-granddaughter," Betty said. "We gonna smoke 'er Friday. Wanna come along?"

"Smoke her?" I asked.

"Smoke 'er up good. Old Amy'll do the ceremony."

"It's a traditional cleansing ritual, Harv," Mike explained. "Nothing secret. It's OK for us to come."

"But . . . no photographs, I suppose."

"Take all them pictures you like," Betty said. "No problem with pictures here."

"On Friday you say?"

"Yup."

"We'll be there."

THE PLACE WAS hubbub, everyone talking at once. I was passed around among the ladies, feeling a bit like a ragdoll. After Betty released me, I found myself being hugged and kissed by full-bodied Sylvia and then by amply endowed Rebecca and then by solid old Betty again. No such luck with curvaceous young Vicki, who sat there serenely nursing Ashley, smiling madonnalike, keeping a proper distance.

Now a warm can of beer was thrust in my hand. The purveyor was old Jack himself, a gruff but sweet-mannered gentleman who focused his heavy-lidded eyes on me.

"You from America?"

"Yup."

"Me, too," he said.

"Really?"

"No crap, mate. Them blackfella you got there, 'em the same as ourself, you know? Like Aboriginal them bloke. I be right at home there with 'm. That's my real home. America. Someday I'm goin' there." He gave a rough, good-humored laugh and subsided back into his chair.

Sylvia looked over at him, one eyebrow raised. "He's a real Dreamtimer, that one," she said.

A thin, elderly woman, the next-door neighbor, nodded like a long-stemmed rose over the elbow-height fence that barely separated Betty and Jack's from the house adjacent. She smiled bemusedly, taking it all in, as much a veranda fixture as the members of the family. This, it turned out, was Biddy.

It was Biddy we'd originally come to see on our way out to Yagga Yagga. She'd earlier told Mike she would take us out "specking"—looking for specks and small nuggets of gold in the nearby gullies—and we'd stopped by to arrange things, but she'd been off somewhere, so we'd chanced upon her next-door neighbor Betty.

Biddy and Betty. To an American ear untuned to Aussie lingo, the two sound pretty much the same, and I'd somehow mistakenly assumed at first that Betty was Biddy and Biddy was Betty, leading to no end of confusion during our first meetings. I soon mended my mistake, but not before becoming faster friends with Betty than Biddy, and I was worried now that Biddy might have taken offense.

"You blokes still goin' speckin' with me?" Biddy asked, her eyes expectant.

As it happened, Betty had also asked us to go gold hunting.

"Oh, sure," I said. "I've even brought along a metal detector. Maybe I'll cadge a nugget, d'you think?"

"Plenty nugget out there," Betty said, intervening. "We'll all go together. Get rich, right?"

She came over and put her two friendly hands on both of our shoulders, Biddy's and mine. Being a healer, she had the knack of soothing every situation with her touch and words. The potential rift between Biddy and me was instantly healed.

"That's right," Biddy said. "We *all* go!"

"First we go get Amy and Munga at Red Hill!" said Betty.

JACK JOHNSTON: *"He's a real Dreamtimer, that one."*

She turned respectfully to Jack, half-dozing in his chair. "Hey, old Jack Johnston, you wanna go?"

"Nah. You blokes go on. Mebbe next time."

THE LADIES WENT to get their gold-specking gear. Young Des, who'd been poring over the copy of *Wisdomkeepers* the whole time, now looked up excitedly. I figured he wanted to go specking, too, but he was pointing at a passage in the book.

"Look here, you blokes," he said. "Listen to what this here Indian medicine man Vernon Cooper has to say."

He read aloud:

> *There's nothing happens to a person that can't be cured. We*
> *come out of the earth, and there's something in the earth to*
> *cure everything. . . . Maybe it takes some herbs. Maybe it*
> *takes some touching. But most of all it takes faith.*

"Sounds like a bloody Aboriginal, doesn't he? And now listen to this."

Des continued:

> *The gift my grandmother passed on is diagnosing and heal-*
> *ing by touch, by laying on of hands. We call it "rubbing." I*
> *rub people with my hands to find the sickness. If the patient*
> *has faith the fever'll come right out, right into my hands.*

"That's what Betty do," old Jack remarked. "She's a toucher, too, that woman." He may have looked asleep, but he'd heard every word. "Them Indian fella, 'em the same as ourself, you know?"

"I thought you said it was the blackfellas," Des said.

"Oh, sure. 'Em too! All of 'm. Same as us. We all American."

Betty and Biddy had returned with their specking gear, which consisted of short lengths of slender rubber hosing and some pieces of wire cable frayed at the ends.

"Scratch'n blow with these," Betty said.

"How's that?" I asked.

She put the hose to her mouth and blew.

"Like that. Blow the sand away. Then brush it with this"—she shook the frayed wire—"and there's the gold!"

She watched my doubtful expression.

"You'll see!" she said.

ON OUR WAY out to pick up Amy and Munga on the outskirts of town, Biddy sat in back and I tucked myself up front between Betty and Mike.

Betty set her hose and wire on the dashboard and took a small plastic vial from her purse. "See what's in here?" she asked. She unscrewed the lid and handed me the vial. I looked inside. Perhaps half an inch of gold flakes gleamed within.

"Plenty more out there!" Betty avowed with assurance, returning the vial to her purse.

"Say, Betty," Mike said, "tell us more about all this healin' by touch. . . . How's that work?"

"I still can't believe the things I do for people," she said. "It's in my hands, in my fingers."

She held her hands in front of her face, flexing her outstretched fingers.

"I don't understand it. Don't know how I got it. People come to me. I just hold 'm and hug 'm and touch 'm all over. I hug 'm well, you know? I feel their body till their body comes back to 'm.

"My healin' comes from the heart," she went on. "I just feel things in my heart. I take their sickness inside my heart and make it better.

"One girl call me while ago. She say come over, her little boy is sick and she don't know what to do. When I go there, he's all stiff, all over his body. I take him and I hold his head, hold his body. I open his mouth and I blow in there three time. I ask him, 'You awright now?' I can feel his body go loose a little. So I blow in his mouth some more, three time more. And I ask him again, 'You awright now?' His body, it's all loose now. He get up and walk around, that li'l fella. Nothin' wrong with 'm anymore.

"Sometime I cry people well. I just hold 'm and we cry and we cry and we cry together. All that cryin' helps heal 'm, I don't know why. There's an old man, he's dyin' in the hospital. The doctors can't do nothin' for 'm. He's gonna die, they say. So I go to the hospital to see 'm. I kiss 'm on the cheek. Sometime that's all they need—a kiss. Sometime they need a little medicine. Bush medicine, you know. So I hug 'm, that poor man, and we cry and cry together. Well, he got up and walk right outa that hospital. He's all healed! I guess we cried that sickness right outa 'm.

"Sometime when someone missin' out in the country, out bush, I cry and cry and cry for 'm and pretty soon here they are, come back home from out bush."

"You think it's the crying that brings 'm back?" I asked.

"Oh sure. It help. I believe it. You gotta *buhLEEVE*, you know? Same with lookin' for that gold nugget. You gotta *buhLEEVE!* 'F you don't *buhLEEVE*, nothin' happen."

WE DROVE UP the driveway to Red Hill, also known as Lunja Aboriginal Community, passing a sign reading "NO GROG AND DRUNKARDS IN THE CAMP—$50 FINE." A litter of beer cans glinted in the hot sun.

"They finish 'm off out here before they go into camp," Mike explained.

We picked up Munga at her house in the compound, then drove across the road to the Warlawurru Catholic school to pick up Amy, whom Mike had described to me as "one of those who carry on the ceremonies, a real Dreamtimer, yet she's a devout Catholic as well."

As we arrived Amy was finishing up a language class in the inner courtyard, surrounded by several dozen Aboriginal children with shining, bright-eyed faces. They were singing a Catholic hymn in "language"—the local Gidja language, in this case. Amy, a wide and squat woman with straight white hair, sat cross-legged in their midst, tapping the concrete floor with the tip of a boomerang, keeping strict and emphatic time. Several children accompanied her with rhythmic clapsticks. The fusion of Catholic hymn and silvery young Aboriginal voices had a lovely and haunting effect.

"I'm grandmother for all of 'm," Amy said, joining us after class was over. "I'm everybody's grandmother."

I installed wide-bodied Amy between Betty and Mike in the front of the car, and, after clearing a space among our clutter of gear, lifted tiny, thin-boned Munga into the back. She seemed to weigh no more than a suit of clothes. Now another lady with two girl toddlers and a naked infant boy asked for a lift into town, and she and her entourage also clambered in back, with me following. Two dogs jumped in as well.

"Them OK, them mine," the lady said.

The naked infant boy wound up in my lap.

"Put these on the li'l fella," the lady said, handing me a tiny pair of shorts.

"Everythin' right with you blokes back there?" Mike called back with an annoying chuckle as we headed into town.

"Oh sure," I said. "Right as rain."

"You say it gonna rain?" the lady asked.

"Uh, no."

The ladies started bantering back and forth in "language," and I absorbed myself in the *here* and *now* of getting those tiny shorts on the writhing boy, who was decidedly unhappy about this Gadia bloke trying to straitjacket him, squirming and howling without cease. Only I seemed to notice. Finally I, too, tuned out. To hell with the *here* and *now*.

THANKFULLY, WE DISGORGED the lady with her three children and two dogs at the roadhouse in town, where I bought an armload of bacon-and-egg sandwiches. That left just Biddy and Munga and myself among the clutter in back—with Betty, Amy, and Mike wedged tight up front. I noticed the ladies snigger, looking my way as I returned with the sandwiches, and I looked down to behold a large wet stain in my lap.

The li'l fella had had his revenge. Retribution from a future Law Man. Take that, you Gadia bloke. I joined belatedly and grudgingly in the general laughter.

After a twenty-minute drive, we bounced off the main road and entered the web of rough tracks beyond the crumbling ruins of Old Halls Creek, site of the first gold rush in Western Australia back in the 1880s. Hardly a square foot of the nearly treeless landscape had not been torn and rubbled, scoured and scraped, dumped and redumped by generations of prospectors. Deep gullies ran their eroded way on either side of the bone-jolting track.

"This way," Betty would say every so often. She was our guide through this desolation, having lived out here with her husband for many years some decades ago. "Now, go that way, take that track." She knew every gully, every hillock.

"See there?" she said, pointing to a spot along the track. "Bloke found 'mself a big nugget there, big as this!"

She held up a clenched fist.

"Maybe we should try right there," I suggested.

"Naw. Keep goin'. I know a place."

I tried to mark the spot in my mind for later reference but soon lost track of it in all that nearly featureless void of fractured and fissured topography. Several times more Betty pointed out sites where nuggets had been found. We drove on for half an hour and finally, at Betty's direction, stopped at the base of an eroded red-dirt hill beside a wide, dry, stony streambed. It looked indistinguishable from scores of other places we had passed.

"This is it!" Betty announced.

The four ladies tumbled out of the car with their rubber hoses and wire scrapers. Mike and I grabbed our metal detectors. Betty seemed to have lost something, searching the front seat and then the back without success.

"Lost my purse!" she said.

We all made a general search, but no purse turned up.

"That the purse with your gold in it?" I asked.

"Yup. And my pension money, too. And my heart tablets!"

I remembered that Betty had come into the roadhouse with me when I'd bought the bacon-and-egg sandwiches. I'd seen her eyeing some fancy hazelnut chocolate bars at the counter and had bought a few for her and the others.

"Maybe you left it at the roadhouse," I suggested.

"Mebbe," she said.

"You want to go right back?"

She shook her head.

"Naw. Go back later. First we get rich!"

Fortunately, she'd left her hose and wire scraper on the dashboard. The ladies dispersed up and down the streambed. Mike and I wandered off with our metal detectors, probing the sands with our mechanical proboscises.

"Make you look like a grasshopper, them things!" Betty laughed as I meandered past her.

The morning heat was up full, and the flies were horrific, crawling in and out of my mouth, nose, and eyes. Only my headphones kept their infernal buzzing out of my ears, and I was grateful for that. Mike, meanwhile, had headed off upstream with the other ladies, leaving Betty and me alone.

"See this?" she called over to me after twenty minutes or so. Glad for an excuse to rest—I hadn't had a single clear signal, only a mind-wearying blur of static—I set down my detector and walked over to her. She was seated in the streambed, crouched low on one elbow, blowing with her rubber hose and scraping away with the wire brush.

"That's one!" she said.

She licked the tip of her little finger, dabbed it in the sand, and held it up to me. Sure enough, there glinted a flake of gold, smaller than a pinhead.

"Good on ya!" I exclaimed in my best Aussie accent.

Carefully she flicked the glistening speck with the tip of her thumbnail into a small tobacco tin.

"See? Gotta *buhLEEVE!*"

I got down on hands and knees and watched closely what she was doing. She'd dug away the sand from a large, lumpish looking blue-gray rock. Firmly anchored in the bottom of the streambed and tilted at an angle, it was layered like slate, but crumbly to the touch.

"See? Mud rock," she said. "That's where the gold is. Got washed in here during floodtime, then got stuck in the mud. Mud turn to rock after that, then get covered with sand again. All you got to do is find that mud rock, then scratch it and blow it, scratch it and blow it, and there it is—you see?—*gold!*"

She dabbed her little finger into the sand again.

Damned if there wasn't another glinting flake!

"I *buhLEEVE!*" I vowed.

CONFIDENCE RENEWED, I returned to my labors. An hour passed. Two. My reward: three rusty nails and a corroded coffee can. I felt beaten. Betty, meanwhile, had added a dozen or so flakes to the growing trove in her tobacco tin. I ambled upstream to check with Mike and the other ladies. I found them all hunched over in the stony streambed, bent at their work. Mike had set aside his metal detector and was on his haunches beside Munga, helping her scoop sand away from a large, exposed mud rock.

"Find anything?" I asked.

"Two old musketballs with the detector," he said. "But look what Munga's found here."

She held up a small bottle with a thin layer of gold flakes and tiny nuggets at the bottom. Amy and Biddy displayed similar results.

Now Mike called out excitedly: "Hey, Harv! Look at this!"

He held his wetted index finger in the air. On it gleamed a golden flake.

"First bloody gold I've ever found!" he exulted.

He stared at it for a few proud moments, then dropped the flake into Munga's bottle.

"I'd just lose it anyway," he said, shrugging.

I made one more half-hour foray with my detector with similar results: an old copper bullet casing and two more rusted nails.

The ladies, meanwhile, continued popping flakes into their bottles and tins. They were absolutely tireless. It was humiliating. At last I switched off my detector and sat dejectedly in the shade of a high bank, leaving my headphones on to keep the blessed flies out of my ears.

"I'm ready to go when you are," I called out.

They continued at their work. I waited. I waited some more. And some more. My whole body ached. I felt drained, depressed, unwanted, unloved.

Now I felt a hand on my shoulder. I'd been drowsing. The hand was cool, firm, comforting. It was Betty's, of course. A healing hand.

"You stopped *buhLEEVin'?*" she asked.

"Yup. For today anyway. You ready to go?"

" 'F you like," she said. "I'll get the others."

Detector in hand, I walked up the bank to the car, eager to get back in that air-conditioned capsule. Mike and the ladies followed me up.

"Find any more?" I asked him.

"Nope. Just that one flake. But Munga here's found a bunch. Amy and Biddy, too."

The four ladies stood outside the car talking about something in "language." There seemed to be a disagreement of some sort. Betty did most of the talking, pleading with them about something. Finally they all nodded, but not without grudging looks in my direction. I wondered what it could be about.

Betty took her little tobacco tin and handed it to the others. Each of them emptied their own trove of gold flakes into the tin. Betty smiled broadly and turned to me, holding the tin in her outstretched hand.

"This for you, old bloke," she said.

I raised a hand in protest.

"Oh, no, please, I couldn't."

She was insistent, adamant.

"We can come here anytime and get gold," she said. "We want you to have it."

She placed it in my hand and closed her palm over mine.

"From all of us to you, old bloke."

I eyed Mike. He nodded. I had no choice but to take it.

"Well, I . . ."

I gave the little tin a gentle shake. The gold made a pleasing sound. I could not restrain a smile. Put all together, the flakes might add up to something the size of a pea.

"What do you think it's worth?" I asked like a fool, betraying my underlying Gadia greed.

Mike squinted an eye at the tin's contents. "Oh . . . maybe thirty, forty dollars . . . maybe more."

I vowed inwardly to make later recompense to my benefactors, but for now I accepted this gleaming gift of their friendship.

I noticed a look of what I took to be slight hurt in Mike's eyes.

"Oh, but, of course, it's for both of us, Mike," I said, handing him the tin.

"No, no . . . no worry, mate . . . wouldn't think of it. It's yours. But . . ." He paused. "You know, you've got the only flake o' gold I ever found in my life in there! Take care of it!"

"I'll sell it to you cheap!" I offered. "That's Gadia's way, isn't it?"

We all laughed. Betty gave me one of her healing hugs, nearly knocking the open tin from my hand. I envisioned its contents scattering back into the sands, back into the Dreamtime. Carefully I closed the lid.

"I *buhLEEVE!*" I announced.

SMOKIN' THE BABY

Smoking the Baby

13

BACK IN TOWN, we stopped at the roadhouse and, sure enough, there was Betty's purse. She'd left it by the cash register when I'd bought the hazelnut chocolate bars. The roadhouse manager had set it behind the counter and now handed it to Betty, who took it with a sweet smile.

"Knew it'd be here," she said.

Without checking the contents, she turned to go.

"Aren't you going to see if the gold and money's still there?" I asked.

"It's there," she pronounced. "No need."

To satisfy this doubting Awtha, she glanced inside. "Yup, all there."

She took out her little vial of gold and gave it a comforting shake, then returned it to the purse. But now, eyebrows raised with sudden concern, she extracted a small plastic pill bottle, opening the lid and staring inside.

"Heart tablets almost gone!" she said, shaking her head. "Been meanin' to get the prescription refilled. Only two left in here. You blokes got time to stop by the pharmacy?"

We walked a few doors down the street to a small store with a pharmaceutical counter.

A thin white man eyed us coolly as we entered. Mike and I stood off to one side while Betty took the pill bottle out of her purse and handed it to him.

He gave the bottle a shake. The two tablets jiggled inside.

"Need some more," Betty said.

He examined the label for several seconds, then shook the bottle again. He looked at Betty with a doubtful eye.

"I got money here," she said.

"Of course you do," he said, dripping condescension. He copied something off the label onto a slip of paper and returned the bottle to Betty.

"Thursday next week," he said. "Outa stock now."

"Oh, I need 'm tomorrow," Betty said. "Only two left. For my heart, you know?"

He gazed down his long nose at her as if she were miles away. A smile smeared his thin, bluish lips.

"Tomorrow's Friday. We don't reorder stock till Tuesday. Come back Thursday. You can pay then."

"But that's a week. Can't be without 'm doctor told me."

"Shoulda ordered earlier then."

"I forgot. Can't you order 'm special?"

"Next Thursday," he repeated flatly.

Mike now entered into it. "Surely you can make a rush order, mate?"

The clerk leveled a disapproving glance at the two of us in our sweat-stained clothes. Disreputable types. Screw 'm.

"Thursday's the best I can do."

"It'd just take a phone call. Wouldn't want somethin' to happen to this lady."

"Ain't my fault. Shoulda ordered earlier."

He swung his gaze from us to Betty. That thin, blue, mocking smile of his hung in the air, disembodied as the Cheshire cat's. He was obviously enjoying this hugely. We'd made his day. I'd gladly have taken a nulla nulla to him.

"Thanks anyway," Mike growled. "Come on, Betty, we'll drive out to the clinic. You can get 'm there."

"Do that," the man said, " 'Bye. Always glad to help. Stop by again."

Mike speared him with a look. "Righto, mate."

We walked out and headed back to the car.

"Bad bloke that one," Betty said.

"Probably has a shelf full o' those bloody pills," Mike muttered, kicking at a stone.

"Bloody wanker," I joined in, repeating a phrase I'd heard in an Aussie pub. I had no idea what it meant, but it somehow seemed appropriate.

Betty looked up at me, hands at her lips, tittering. "Oh, you a funny bloke, you old man!"

"Why? What did I say?"

Mike leaned over, smothering a smile with his hand, and whispered something obscenely scatological into my ear.

"Oh," I said, embarrassed. "Sorry, Betty. But, damn it, that's what he bloody *is!*"

She gave me one of her healing hugs, and we all burst out laughing.

Betty got her tablets at the clinic.

NEXT MORNING WE drove out to "smoke the baby."

"I like smokin' the baby," Betty said. "It's the start of her *real* life."

Amy chose a spot north of town, the sandy bank of a dry streambed shaded by river gums.

"Plenty konkerberry bush round here," she announced. "Got to make the fire with konkerberry. Get the dry wood first, then the green leaves. Wood to make the fire, leaves to make the smoke."

She fell on her knees and started scooping a hole for a pit fire in the sand.

"Go on, you blokes." Her sandpapery voice was gentle but firm. She was in charge here, there was no doubt of that.

While Vicki stood by nursing little Ashley, Mike and I gathered dry konkerberry wood, and Betty picked an armload of fresh green leaves. This konkerberry bush, a scrawny but solid tree with orange-streaked yellow wood, had medicinal properties, Mike explained.

"Grows all over the Kimberley. Very common, really. The Aboriginals are really keen on it. Use it as a medicine for curing colds and other things. Inhale the smoke, that's the thing. Also make a tonic out of it, grind up the bark and leaves and twigs and boil it up. There's also a berry you can eat certain times o' year. But the smoke's the main thing. Gettin' smoked with konkerberry is the start of the baby's ceremonial life. It's a cleansing, a kind of purification. And not just for babies. I've been smoked a few times myself. It's a great honor. They use it for all sorts of things, a cure-all. If a mother's havin' trouble gettin' her milk to flow, then they smoke her breasts."

We carried our armloads of dry wood back to Amy. Betty followed with the green leaves. Amy crouched on her knees before the fire pit, swaying meditatively back and forth, humming under her breath, her strong hands steadily creating layers of kindling. Now a match was produced, and a thin tendril of smoke curled up. A lovely, incenselike pungency instantly permeated the air, reminiscent of the soul-invigorating smell of sage and sweet grass I'd experienced at Native American ceremonies.

The fire took hold, starting to crackle, but immediately Amy sprinkled mineral water over it from a plastic bottle, dampening the flames. Now she set a batch of green konkerberry leaves in the fire, sticking her head into the sudden white smoke and blowing mightily with wide-puffed cheeks.

A cloud of white smoke arose, and the pungency in the air increased tenfold.

"Now bring the baby!" Amy said.

Vicki brought the wide-eyed Ashley, only in diapers now, and set her in Amy's lap. Pouring water from the plastic bottle into her cupped hand, Amy applied it liberally to the baby's hair, head, chest, back, and legs.

"Don't wanna burn her," she explained.

MOTHER VICKI,
BABY ASHLEY, AND DOTING
GRANDMOTHER BETTY:
"It's the start of her real life."

Ashley made no cry, not even a whimper. I'll never forget that look in her wide-brown Dreamtime eyes as Amy held her out directly into the perfumed smoke like a living sacrifice.

The smoke enveloped her tiny form.

For perhaps twenty seconds Amy held her there. Finally, she extracted the child from the smoke and rocked her in her arms. Ashley smiled sweetly, cooing.

"Done," Amy announced. "All done."

It was over. No words, no prayers had been spoken. I suppose they would have been irrelevant. The act itself was the prayer.

Vicki took Ashley from Amy's arms, gave the baby a triumphant kiss, and headed back to the car with her. I turned to follow when I heard Amy's commanding voice.

"Now *you*." Her eyes were on me. She beckoned with one hand.

"Don't you wanna be smoked? Be good for you! Come on! Good for headache. Good for everythin'!"

BETTY PICKING
KONKERBERRY LEAVES FOR
SMOKIN' THE BABY

I didn't hesitate. I could use a good soul-cleansing, God knew.

I walked back and stood before her. Cupping her hands, she dipped them into the still-rising konkerberry smoke, then applied the smoke to my head, face, shoulders, rubbing it lightly up and down my body, even down to my feet.

"Washin' you with the smoke, see?" Amy said. "Clean up your soul!"

I drank in the smoke, feeling its pungency enter me.

Betty stood a few feet off watching with approval.

"Gotta *buhLEEVE!*" she intoned, smiling maternally.

"There!" Amy said, applying the last of the smoke. "You been smoked, old bloke!"

"Feelin' better?" Mike asked, dousing the fire with the remaining mineral water and covering the remains with sand.

"None the worse," I said.

Back at the car Betty gave me a solid hug. She gazed on me with motherly pride.

"Now"—she smiled—"you start your *real* life!"

JACK ROGERS:

"a truly glorious man"

Dreamtime Blues

14

A SMALL AND wiry Aboriginal man with a tight gray ruff of beard and a jaunty step waved us down the next morning in front of the motel pub.

"It's old Jack Rogers!" Mike said, pulling the car to a stop and getting out to speak to the man.

The two embraced warmly.

"Hey, Harv," Mike called out. "C'mon shake hands with an old friend of mine. Old Jack Rogers himself."

I reached through the car window and shook Jack's strong, bony hand. He peered in at me with smiling curiosity. His handsome, well-chiseled face beamed friendliness.

"Saw him dancin' up a storm at the corroboree last month," Mike said. "Isn't that right, Jack?"

"Oh yeah. Dance up a storm awright. Plenty fun that one."

"Any more corroborees goin' on now, Jack?"

"Naw. None now. Say, which way you blokes goin'?" he asked.

"On our way to Fitzroy."

He asked for a lift out to Yiyilu, an Aboriginal community a hundred kilometers or so west of Halls Creek on the main high-way to Fitzroy Crossing, our next destination.

"You bet, mate," Mike replied.

And so we threw in our lot for the day with Jack and Ray Rogers and their friend Bob Jack. We arranged to pick up Jack and Bob Jack an hour later and then drive out to the edge of town to pick up Jack's "big brother," Ray.

"Lively bunch o' blokes," Mike told me, returning to the car. "Not Law Men or anythin', but they hang on to the old ways best they can. You've gotta see old Jack get all painted up and do his dance. You won't believe the transformation! Becomes a different bloke altogether. That ceremonial paint turns him into a truly glo-rious man. And his brother Ray plays a mean didgeridoo!"

Soon the five of us were tooling along the main highway to Yiyilu, Mike and I up front, the three of them jammed in back where they'd insisted on sitting together, and now were singing loudly and beating out syncopated rhythms on the Eski lid.

"The boys are feelin' a bit sparky!" Mike chuckled. "Must be the Wet season!"

Jack's brother Ray kept saying, "Need me didgeridoo! Need me didgeridoo!"

"You got one at Yiyilu?" I asked him.

"Mebbe borrow one at the souvenir shop!" he said. "I'll play 'm for you when we get there."

"Maybe you fellas'll do a dance for the Awtha here when we get there," Mike suggested.

"Oh yeah. We'll do 'm a dance!" Jack agreed, pounding out an Aboriginal rhythm on the back of my headrest. He let out a loud wail in a scratchy tenor voice—"*Yahhh . . . aahhhhhh*"—while Ray, cupping his hands to his mouth, mimicked the guttural dronings of a didgeridoo—"*ðu-DUH-ðu-ree-loonggg, ðu-DUH-ðu-ree-loonggg.*"

Bob Jack, meanwhile, clapped and yahooed with abandon.

The music crescendoed. Mike pounded the steering wheel as he drove. I was knocking out a beat on the dashboard while Jack's syncopations intensified on the back of my headrest so that the Aboriginal rhythms seemed to be coming in stereo right out of my throbbing mind. The whole car became a corroboree.

Finally the singing faded out. We were an hour and a half out of Halls Creek, nearly to Yiyilu. Jack, Ray, and Bob Jack subsided into contented laughter in back, talking in a mixture of

JACK AND RAY STRIKE UP
AN IMPROMPTU CONCERT
WITH DIDGERIDOO:

*"∂u-DUH-∂u-ree-loonggg . . .
Ehhhh! Ehhhh! Ehhhhhhhhh!"*

English and "language" among themselves.

Their conversation rose and fell, swelling after a time into what seemed to be an argument of some kind between Jack and Ray. As best I could make out, they were talking about their father. "No bloody good that man!" Ray blurted out angrily.

"He done what he could," said Jack defensively.

Jack noticed us listening.

"Hey, old bloke," he said, tapping my elbow. "Turn on that radio again, will ya?"

I turned the radio on to some music.

"Louder, mate, d'you mind?"

I turned the volume up high, and Jack and Ray resumed their argument in privacy.

AT YIYILU, A neat community of well-built tin-roofed houses, Ray borrowed a brightly painted didgeridoo from the souvenir shop, and we returned to the veranda of Jack's little house for an impromptu concert. Ray, however, could get only a hoarse bleat out of the souvenir didgeridoo.

"No damn good this stick. Got a crack in 'm." He snorted. He went back to the souvenir shop, got another didgeridoo, cursed that one as well, and finally retrieved a third. Pressing this firmly to his clenched lips and puffing until the tendons in his thin neck stood out taut, he finally managed to coax out a pulsating drone that sounded like a swarm of flies in the ear. Jack hovered over him, picking up the incipient rhythm and urging it along with loud claps of his hands. Bob Jack grabbed a flat throwing stick and slapped it sharply against his thigh. Several children gathered around, clapping in time.

"*Ahhhhh . . . Ooooohhh . . . Ahhhh . . . Ooooohhhh . . .*" came Jack's piercing, high-pitched voice.

"*Ehhhh! Ehhhh! Ehhhhhhhhh!*"

Ray continued bellowing away at the didgeridoo with swollen cheeks, sustaining the rhythm for perhaps two minutes. Then the buzzing drone broke off suddenly and out came a pitiful, dying squeal, as if a baby goat were being strangled. The singing and clapping ended abruptly.

Ray, rolling his eyes, stopped blowing and glared at the didgeridoo with contempt.

"Bloody tourist rubbish!" He shook his head in defeat. "Looks like no more didgin' today, you blokes," he said. "Sorry. Gettin' tired anyway."

Both he and Jack looked heavy lidded, stifling yawns.

"Spark's wearin' off," Mike said, catching my eye.

The corroboree was over.

"Mebbe you'll paint up for the Awtha here, Jack?"

"Mebbe," Jack muttered. He looked peeved. I could see he didn't want to do it.

"It's not necessary, Jack," I volunteered, feeling that old gnawing at the ragged edges of my Gadia conscience.

"You come back tomorrow," he said. "We do it then. Go get white ocher up on the hill, OK? Too tired now."

He and Ray still seemed out of sorts with each other.

Ray came up to Mike. "Goin' back Halls Creek now, right? I gotta get back."

"If that's what you want, mate."

BEFORE WE LEFT, Bob Jack insisted we come over to his house to see his paintings. He showed us several small canvases, one of which particularly caught my eye—a pointillist thing in blue, brown, and white showing a swirl of tentacles enclosing some spermlike squiggles.

"What are these?" I asked him, pointing to the tentacles.

"Oh, them Law Men, you know?"

I pointed to the squiggles. "And these?"

"Boys. Them boys. See, the Law Men them puttin' their arms around the boys, gatherin 'm in, teachin 'm the Law. That's in the long long time ago."

"You make it up, that story?" I asked.

"Oh no. Old people they tell me that story. It's Dreamtime story, you know?"

I stood there considering it. It was quite lovely, really—painted with thousands of small dots.

"Must have taken a long time to paint it."

"Oh yeah. One day. One whole day."

He eyed me narrowly. "You gonna buy it, mate?"

"Errr . . . well . . . how much you askin', Bob Jack?" My resolve was weakening.

His face contracted in thought for a long moment. Then, drawing in his breath with a slight whistle—obviously expecting some argument—he intoned, "Twenty dollar."

I had seen works no superior selling in urban galleries for twenty or thirty times that. I fought off the primordial surge of capitalism in my Gadia breast. The painting could be had, I guessed, for fifteen, even ten dollars. Bob Jack seemed definitely intent on selling it. To refuse to buy it would be an insult. Idiotic, as well. I gave in, deciding it would be obscene to bargain him down. Twenty dollars quickly changed hands. The painting was *mine*. That gathering of Law Men in the Dreamtime was now Gadia property. The guilt stuck in my throat.

"Thought you said you weren't goin' to buy anythin'," Mike said.

A guilt-assuaging thought came into my mind.

"Here's a little piece of the Dreamtime from the Awtha to you," I said, presenting the painting to Mike. "That'll look nice on your wall at home, don't you think?"

"No doubt, mate."

He seemed surprised but pleased, accepting it with a delighted smile. Not a shred of guilt in his eyes. My own guilt faded. And Bob Jack, well—damn it—Bob Jack had his twenty bucks and seemed much the happiest of the three of us.

"I suppose I could have had it for fifteen or even ten," I remarked as we walked back to the car.

"For sure," Mike said. "But Bob Jack's happy as a clam."

Maybe for once I had inadvertently done the right thing.

NEXT MORNING, STOPPING off again at Yiyilu on our way to Fitzroy Crossing, we climbed a steep, gravelly, red-rock ridge with Jack to what he called "the ocher place." Out of a small pit near the ridgeline he scooped a handful of blindingly white ocher, putting it in a plastic bag.

"Plenty sacred this place," he said.

"Any Dreamtime story about it, Jack?" I asked.

"Oh yeah. Must be. Always a Dreamtime story."

Jack seemed in a somber mood, untalkative. Yesterday's shine had dimmed. He was obviously sorry he'd agreed to "paint up" for this prying Awtha but was going through the motions out of politeness.

"Can't really do it," he said as we came down the hill.

"Can't do what, Jack?"

"Paint up right. Only do that for ceremony, you know?"

"Maybe you can just daub some paint on?" I persisted in my obscene Gadia way. I didn't want him to fake anything. And yet I did.

"Oh sure." He shrugged.

With a small stick, he mixed some of the white ocher and a splash of water in a shoe polish tin and, eyes sad as those of a Ringling Brothers clown, slowly smeared the gleaming pigment on his face and chest.

Even this jaded Awtha was feeling bad about what we were doing. This was a desecration we'd forced him into. And yet—the effect was striking. The crude daubs of white paint had somehow instantly transformed him. This wiry little man, so comically "sparky" yesterday, so downcast and apologetic just a few moments ago, now looked back at me through my camera lens with a ferocious dignity, nostrils quivering, eyes fearless and calm. He radiated power and serenity.

The "truly glorious man" Mike had spoken of was suddenly there before us. He'd always been there, of course. That paint hadn't changed anything, only made what had always been there momentarily visible to this otherwise eyeless Gadia.

I remember how I'd often unconscionably and impudently asked Native American elders to "dress up" in their ceremonial garb. In particular, I will never forget Lakota elder Mathew King's reply to my request one day to see him in his "war bonnet."

"White Man always gets everything wrong," he'd told me, piercing me with his eyes,

> He calls us savages, but he's the savage. See, he calls
> this headdress a war bonnet. Sure, we used it in war, but
> most of the time it was for ceremony. Every feather
> stands for a good deed, and I have thirty-six in mine. It's
> not about war; it's about who we are. When we sing
> songs he calls them war songs. But they're not war songs,
> they're prayers to God. We have drums, so White Man
> calls them war drums; but they're not for war, they're
> for talking to God. There's no such thing as a war drum.
> He sees how our warriors paint their faces, so he calls
> it war paint. But it's not for war, it's to make it so God
> can see our faces clearly if we have to die.

Jack Rogers's eyes, framed by the crude daubs of sacred white ocher, stared at me through the camera lens. They skewered my Gadia soul.

I took my bloody photographs, simultaneously shamed and shameless.

"Awright, you blokes," Jack said. "Gotta go now."

We drove him back to Yiyilu, where an Aboriginal man crossing the compound caught a glimpse of Jack's white-daubed face through the car window.

"Hey! Look! Old Jack's painted himself up pretty!" he called out in derision.

Jack slid down in his seat, cringing with embarrassment.

I felt wretched. And I was.

Jack made his escape from our company, and Mike and I headed toward Fitzroy Crossing.

"Maybe I shouldn't be doing all this," I lamented to Mike, aching inside.

"Sure you should, mate. What you're doin' is important. You're seein' through all the crap to these people's dignity. That's well worth doin' to my mind."

I was less than convinced.

We drove on.

BUNABA ELDER BILLY OSCAR:

"My real name Mowanbun."

Pigeon Dreaming

15

WE WERE ON the trail of a ghost—the elusive shade of Pigeon, or Jandamarra, the "outlaw" of the Bunaba tribe who staged a three-year revolt against white authority in the Kimberley back in the 1890s and whose spirit, local Aboriginals swear, still haunts the subterranean cavern of Tunnel Creek in the Napier Range.

At the Junjuwa community in Fitzroy Crossing, we looked up Bunaba elder Billy Oscar, one of the keepers of the Pigeon story. He looked at us doubtfully when we asked him to drive with us out to Tunnel Creek.

"Mmmm," he said, rubbing his white-grizzled chin. "Mebbe you better talk with Banjo Woorunmarra in Derby. He know that story better'n me."

"It was Banjo who told us to look you up," Mike explained. "I rang him up in Derby yesterday. We'll be seeing him in a few days. He said maybe you could show us around."

"Well . . . I dunno. Gotta ask the council first."

The Junjuwa council deliberated on the matter and decided that one of its members, an engaging and well-spoken young man named Patrick Green, would accompany us for the day trip to Tunnel Creek with Billy.

"What exactly you blokes looking for?" Patrick asked.

"The Awtha here wants to put Pigeon's story in his book," Mike replied.

"You could say we're lookin' for his ghost," I added.

"Mebbe trouble for you 'f you find 'm," Billy commented.

"How so?" I asked.

"Pigeon be watchin' you 'f you come see 'm. He still walk around there, in the cave, you know? Too many tourist there. He gotta hide. Don't like all them whitefella. He be watchin' though. Mebbe don't wanna be in your book. Mebbe point the bone at you blokes."

"I'll be respectful," I said.

His eyes studied me. Pryin' whitefella. Gotta watch 'm.

A TWO-HOUR DRIVE took us through some of the most stunningly beautiful country in the Kimberley, a stark and wide-angled landscape of flatland scrub and spinifex interrupted by sudden low but spectacular mountains—the Oscar, Napier, and King Leopold ranges, remnants of a coral barrier reef 350 million years old. Uplifted by tectonic forces from the sea and shoved far inland over the eons, these fractured and discolored limestone massifs have been scoured and whittled by countless Wets into a wonderland of deep gorges and marvelously sculptured rock formations.

BILLY BECAME EXCITED as we approached the upthrusting blue phalanx of the Oscar Range.

"That's where my name come from, them hills. Oscar, you know?"

"You were named after the mountains, Billy?"

"My real name Mowanbun," he said, "but I'm called Billy

Oscar. Used to be Oscar Station out here. I was born old Oscar homestead long time ago. Must be eighty year ago. I be a stockman long time there, but all gone now that place. No more cattle there. No more old people out there. . . . Oh, and you blokes see that gorge there? My father used to take me there to cut bamboo for spears. Good water there.

"This country all Bunaba country," he enthused, pointing out landmark after landmark with an owner's pride. "But right here, this part here, this Manjari country, you know?"

Patrick explained: "What he means is that this whole country is Bunaba territory, but this particular part of it, right around here, belongs to the Manjari family. There are families within the Bunaba people. Manjari is Billy's family group. He's the eldest of the family. So this is Manjari country. This is his home. He's the owner here."

Billy pointed a finger to a low hill in the distance. "Old people die here by this hill, and we had a funeral. I have a place on that hill for when I pass away."

A bit farther on he pointed to some holes in a high rock wall.

"That place is . . ." He paused and turned to Patrick.

"Should I tell 'm about Dreamtime places?"

"OK, sure. A little bit maybe."

"See," Billy went on, "this place . . . in the Dreamtime, the Dingo he scratch them holes. . . . And that one, see that big tall rock up there? That's the . . ."

Once again he paused. He and Patrick conversed in "language" for a few moments, shaking their heads.

"Mebbe that one I don't tell," Billy said finally. "Man story, you know? Maybe woman they read your book. Not s'pose tell 'm that story. Not for woman. Man story only that one."

"You can tell *me*," Mike offered.

Billy cupped his hand and whispered into Mike's ear for a couple of minutes. The two of them repeatedly chuckled, grinning widely.

• •

Mike glanced my way. "Plenty good story that one. But don't tell the Awtha here. He'd just put it in his book."

"No, really, I wouldn't," I protested.

"It's a bit phallic, Harv. Damn interesting, actually. But definitely not for the book."

Mike later told me the story, and, entertaining though it might be to some, I will honor my promise not to repeat it here.

WE DROVE ON through a series of fractured massifs.

"Here Manjari country stop," announced Billy as we approached the Napier Range. "From here on it's Banjo's country. Different family than Manjari. He belong same family as Jandamarra. Pigeon, you know? They call him Pigeon 'cause—*phfft!*—soon as you see 'm he's gone, just like pigeon in the bush, he disappear—*phfft!*—you can't find 'm. He was a Bunaba man. I tell you little bit o' that Pigeon story, but Banjo he tell you a lot more if you ask 'm.

"Old people bin tell me that story. Jandamarra, he bin runnin' all the time in that country, runnin' from the coppers. They comin' to kill 'm 'cause he shoot that bloody constable. They chase 'm but he go cave to cave. Run inside the cave then run out other side. Always get away, that Jandamarra. Magic man, you know? Too smart for them coppers. They shoot 'm but they can't kill 'm."

I knew the story's outline from the history books. In the 1880s and 1890s white settlers pushed into this remote region, laying claim to the lands of the Bunaba and other Aboriginal peoples, shooting those who resisted and shunting others into forced labor on stations and missions. All those left in the "wild" were considered outlaws.

Jandamarra, a young Bunaba man caught up in all of this, was arrested for sheep spearing and avoided prison or worse by becoming a tracker for the police, reluctantly hunting down his own people. One day in 1894, the story goes, he shot his boss, a constable named William Richardson, and unchained a group of black prisoners he had just hunted down, fleeing with them into bush. For three years, in what became known to history as Pigeon's War, he and his followers eluded a small army of determined pursuers, hiding in caves and emerging periodically to spear a sheep or stage hit-and-run raids on white settlements.

A man of towering bravado, feared by white and black alike, Jandamarra enjoyed nothing more than toying with his pursuers, leading them on wild chases and then suddenly appearing in plain sight—just out of rifle range—on a cliff high above, stark naked, shaking his rifle and spear in the air. Taunting them from afar, he would then disappear again—*"phfft!"* as Billy would put it—into the network of caves honeycombing the area. Finally, in 1897, already badly wounded from a gun battle with police a short time before, he was ambushed near Tunnel Creek by a fellow black tracker and shot dead at close range.

"Take a blackfella to catch a blackfella," Billy said.

Some say that his head was blown away, others that his skull was taken to Perth to be put on display. Fact became legend, and legend swelled into epic myth, elevating Jandamarra to the status of a Dreamtime hero among the Bunaba people, who pass down his exploits from generation to generation.

WE REACHED THE rockbound entrance to Tunnel Creek, where Jandamarra had been heading when the trackers finally found and dispatched him. Out of the boulder-littered cave mouth came a steady, cool breeze, cutting the midday heat.

"Plenty plenty place to hide in here," Billy said, peering into the shadowy, high-ceilinged cavern gouged out of the limestone by the floods of countless millenniums. "That creek bin goin' right inside the rocks, right inside the hill. Jandamarra hide up them high rock, you know? He look down. You can't see 'm, but Jandamarra he see you."

Mike and I had slogged barefoot through the knee-deep water

on a previous visit, probing the 2,500-foot tunnel's pitch dark passages until we came to a kind of inner cathedral where the ceiling had collapsed, allowing golden spears of sunlight from above into the cavernous gloom. It's said that the Rainbow Snake created this hole in the cave's roof and that, somewhere in a deep underwater abyss hereabouts, the great serpent still sleeps, awaiting resurrection in a Dreamtime yet to come.

I could envision Jandamarra hiding out in here, feeding off a leg of pilfered mutton on a high ledge, silently watching for his pursuers, perhaps stealing out from time to time to retouch the ancient sacred images of the Rainbow Snake and the Wandjina on nearby rock walls, thus assuring the return of the life-giving Wet. He was, after all, a fully initiated Law Man, a "clever man of high degree," conversant with the sacred mysteries and rituals.

This place reeked of the Dreamtime.

"Jandamarra didn't die," Billy reaffirmed. "He go into the water, his spirit did."

He poked his finger through the mirror surface of the still pool, setting up ripples that dashed his reflection.

"Sometime," Billy said, "sometime you see his face in the water. He look up at you, watchin', watchin'. . . . I don't see 'm now. He musta bin gone somewhere else for now."

MIKE ASKED BILLY if he was familiar with a Wandjina rock-art site high in the cliffs a few kilometers down the road. Billy shook his head.

"Nope. None there I know 'bout. You been there?"

"Many times," Mike acknowledged. "C'mon, I'll show you blokes."

We drove to the site, another of Mike's "secret places," and climbed a rocky scree up to a high red-rock overhang whose arched ceiling glowed with haloed Wandjina and other figures. If Tunnel Creek had been a cathedral of the Dreamtime, this was a chapel. Billy seemed amazed at finding the place, staring wide-eyed at the extensive artwork, faded but still distinct. He ran the tips of his fingers lovingly along some deep-grooved scratches in the wall.

"Them old people sharpen their spear here, see?"

Under a large, full-length Wandjina figure at the center of the overhang, he gazed upward reverently.

"Come from the wind that Wandjina," he said. "Bring 'm the rain, you know?"

Now Billy placed his open-palmed hands directly against the rock wall and closed his eyes, falling into a rapt meditation, his mouth moving silently. He stood there with his back to us for more than a minute, head nodding occasionally as if in response to some inner voice. Finally he turned around, a gentle smile playing on his lips.

"Jandamarra been here," he said softly. "Jandamarra been here not so long ago. Mebbe we just miss 'm."

ON THE WAY back to Fitzroy, we noticed a billowing cloud of red dust approaching us along the wide dirt road. Out of the cloud materialized a battered truck carrying half a dozen Aboriginal stockmen.

"It's the mob from Leopold Downs!" Patrick said. "C'mon, we'll have a yarn with 'm!"

They seemed a rough but friendly bunch, plainly happy to see Billy and Patrick. It turned out they were on their way back to the Leopold Downs Station homestead after a day mustering wild bulls. Red dust powdered their faces and clothes.

"Just trucked off a hundred twenty-five head to the meat works at Katherine," said a burly man named Kevin, obviously the boss.

"It's a big success story, Leopold Downs Station," Patrick said. "Kevin here's the station manager, you know? ATSIC helped us buy the land. Bought back our own ancestral country. People said we could never make it a working station, that we'd run it into the ground. But we're provin 'm wrong. No better stockmen and horsemen than Aboriginals."

Patrick introduced Mike and the Awtha to the boys, showing them a copy of *Wisdomkeepers,* which Kevin immediately appropriated, leaning against the side of the truck and flipping through the pages. "Bloody interesting these Indians," he said.

Billy engaged the others, telling them excitedly of the hitherto unknown Wandjina cave down the road. They stood around talking in "language," making quick work of all the candy, snacks, and soda pop we had left. The late afternoon sun poured down, sculpturing their features into glowing dark bronze. Mike and I grabbed our cameras to capture the scene.

"Hey, listen to this, you mob," Kevin said.

He read aloud from the chapter on Lakota chief Mathew King:

When we want wisdom we go up the hill and talk to God.
Four days and four nights, without food and water. Yes,
you can talk to God up on a hill by yourself. You can say
anything you want. Nobody's there to listen to you.
That's between you and God and nobody else. It's a great
feeling to be talking to God. I know. I did it way up on the
mountain. The wind was blowing. It was dark. It was
cold. And I stood there and I talked to God.

Everyone fell silent. The echo of Mathew's words hung on the air. In the distance a flock of white cockatoos settled for the night into the upper branches of a boab, their raucous cries thin and eerie on the wind. A chill raced down my spine. The images of Mathew King and Jandamarra somehow converged in my mind. A strange, imponderable connection had been struck. Wounded Knee had come to the Kimberley.

I remembered some other words Mathew King had spoken that long-ago day in 1984:

I'm an Indian. I'm one of God's children. . . .
I don't believe in violence.
But if I take my guns I can do a lot of damage.
I'm a warrior. I'll fight till they kill me!

Jandamarra would have understood that.

The mob from Leopold Downs was visibly moved. I was glad I'd saved those words of Mathew's, respoken with such effect so many years later, here at the edges of the Dreamtime. It made me feel better about what I was doing.

Even a bloody Awtha has his occasional uses in this world.

Bunaba elder Banjo Woorunmarra:

"We're the owners of this land."

Keeper of the Dream

A MASSIVE BOAB of a man, Bunaba elder Banjo Woorunmarra—principal keeper of the Jandamarra story—balanced his great bulk with both hands on the bare mattress as he sat up from the sagging iron bedstead, his cane and battered wide-brim drover's hat at his bare feet on the concrete floor.

"I've had a bad leg," he said in an apologetic voice, wheezing with effort. "Got all swollen. Gettin' better now, but it's still hard to move about."

"Please, don't get up, Banjo."

"Get 'm some chair, these blokes!" he snapped out, and one of the women on the veranda slid a couple of plastic chairs our way. At a sidelong glance from Banjo, the small crowd that had been gathered around him at our arrival melted away, except for one extremely dark-skinned young man, dashingly handsome in a black cowboy hat, who leaned casually against a wooden post on the other side of the veranda, contemplating us with steady, non-committal eyes.

"So you wanna hear Jandamarra story," Banjo said. "That's good. Sit up close, you two. Here, you, get me that bag down there."

He pointed to a large, scuffed leather handbag on the floor beside the bed. I handed it up to him, surprised at its weight.

"That's my dilly bag," Banjo said, smiling. "Jus' like a woman's. Got everythin' in there, you know?"

He unsnapped the latch and rummaged inside, producing a small zipper bag, from which he extracted a plastic vial.

"Medicine for the leg," he explained.

Throwing back his head, he gulped down a pill, then returned the vial to the zipper bag and the zipper bag to the handbag.

Now he rummaged in the handbag once again, finally coming up with a small black leatherette case. I thought of the sacred board Reg Birch had produced a few weeks before from his black briefcase, and now half-expected Banjo to extract some amulet or other sacred item from the little case, but the object within turned out, mundanely, to be a pink-plastic hearing aid. This Banjo fitted carefully into one ear, spending several seconds adjusting it. A shrill whistling sound emitted from his ear. Banjo tapped the hearing aid repeatedly, annoyance in his eyes.

"Bloody thing. Batteries low."

"We'll pick up some new ones for you," Mike offered.

"That be good o' you blokes." Banjo nodded.

He gave the hearing aid another sharp tap with his fingernail. The whistling died. He nodded again and turned his attention to us.

"Now then. Jandamarra . . . I been gonna tell you his story. He was a Bunaba man. That's my people, you know. We're the owners of this land. White man come here, take our land, stole it. . . . We didn't raise our hand, but we got killed in our own country. White man, he don't want to share with the blackfella. He want it all. He's too greedy. Gotta fill his pockets. He take everything, whitefella does. But *we* own the land!

"Me, I understand white people. I work with 'm, live with 'm all my life. Work with whitefellas out drovin'. Drove four thousand head o' cattle all the way to Queensland, just four of us, two blackfella and two whitefella. Got plenty close, them and me. Eat with 'm, drink with 'm, sleep next to 'm out bush. So I know these whitefella. I know how they think. We talk-talk to each other, you know?

"But in those day blackfellas don't understand whitefellas and whitefella don't understand blackfella. In those day blackfella's nothin' but a slave. It was hard. There was nothin' good. If blackfella been workin' and drag their feet they shoot 'm like dog.

"But missionaries didn't want 'm to kill 'm. They want those youngfella come to mission and live there, go to school, go to church, become like whitefella. So p'lice they go out and get blackfella trackers to track 'm down some blackfella for mission, put 'm in chain and handcuff. If they don't wanna go—*poof*—they shoot 'm."

Banjo tapped the hearing aid, which was whistling again.

"Too much noise," he said. "Hard to hear, hard to talk."

NOW THE YOUNG man in the black cowboy hat walked over to us.

"Excuse me," he said. "You don't mind if I interfere? I'm Banjo's grandson. I was just wonderin' what you two are here for."

He put one arm protectively around Banjo's shoulder.

"This here's my grandson Terence," Banjo said. "He's a rodeo rider. Terence, meet Harvey and Mike. Harvey's an Awtha. Writin' a book about Aboriginal people."

"Oh."

Terry's dark eyes probed me, distrusting.

"Banjo was just about to tell us the Pigeon story," I explained. "But he's been having trouble with his hearing aid."

Terence maintained his hand on Banjo's shoulder.

"Lotta white blokes come around here," he said. "Askin' lotta questions. Tourists, they're the worst. Gotta watch 'm. While back we buried some old people in a cave near here, and the tourists come along and they steal the bones. For souvenirs, you know. Can you imagine? We try to find 'm, but they got away."

"Bloody wankers," Mike said.

"Yeh, bloody wankers awright. So we just like to know who's comin' round here, you know? Gotta be careful. Don't want people takin' things that don't belong to 'm."

"No problem with Banjo tellin' us the Pigeon story, is there?" I asked.

"Oh, no. That's his job. He's the one to ask. Pigeon's our family, you know. I'm part of his blood. And Banjo, too. Banjo's Pigeon's grandson and I'm Banjo's grandson, so we're all one blood."

"Yeah, Pigeon's my grandfather," Banjo confirmed.

"That's why I'm such a good rodeo rider," Terence went on. "I got Pigeon in me. He knew horses, Pigeon did. Banjo used to be a pretty good horse rider, too. We got horse ridin' in our blood. We both got Pigeon in us."

"So whereabouts you been ridin', Terence?" Mike asked.

Terence's hand slipped off Banjo's shoulder. He seemed to be warming up to us.

"I became a champion buck and bull rider in Broome last year. Got five hundred dollars in cash. And last weekend I won saddle bronc in Turkey Creek. People say I'm pretty bloody good."

"He's the best there is," Banjo declared. "He's a good boy, my grandson here."

Now Banjo cleared his throat.

"Terry," he said in a gentle but authoritative tone, "these

blokes'n me we're talkin'. You leave us till we're finished, you hear?"

"No worry, Grandpa," Terence said respectfully. "I was just makin' sure everythin's right with you and these blokes here."

He tipped the brim of his black cowboy hat.

"He's askin' me to leave and I'm leavin'. Catch you later. G'day, you mates."

Smiling deferentially, he ambled off.

"Good boy he is," Banjo said. "But sometime he talk too much. Shouldn't interfere with elders, you know?"

"Perfectly understandable," I said. "He just wanted to check us out."

The whistling resumed from his earpiece. Banjo winced. "Need those bloody battery. Can't talk now."

Mike offered to bring some new batteries in the morning.

"Good," Banjo said. "We have a good talk-talk then."

JANDAMARRA'S STORY

Next morning, with the new batteries installed and Banjo's hearing aid back in working order, we drove to the outskirts of Derby to continue our conversation in the shade of the famous Prison Tree, a thousand-year-old boab with an enormous, hollow trunk.

"Old days," Banjo explained, sitting down at the foot of the tree, "them p'lice fella use this boab tree for a jail. Stop here to rest comin' back to Derby with all them blackfella chained up, the ones they catch spearin' sheep or cattle. Put 'm inside the boab, maybe ten or fifteen people inside there. Jandamarra, he work for the p'lice, you know? He track down his own people. The coppers they make 'm do it or else they put 'm in jail 'mself for spearin' sheep.

"Constable Richardson, he was the one that cause all the

humbug. He start all the trouble. He was Jandamarra's mate when they're boys. Oh, yeah, they're good mates they are. Then Richardson, they make him p'lice fella constable and he tell Jandamarra, 'Hey, mate, you come workin' with me, you be my friend.' So Jandamarra he goes workin' for Richardson, trackin' down blackfella, catchin' his own people and put 'm in chain. Blackfella they call Jandamarra 'white man dog' 'cause he hunt down his own people. That's at Lillamooloora, the p'lice station, right by Windjana Gorge.

"One day Jandamarra he go off catchin' big mob o' blackfella, put 'm in chains and handcuff, you know? While he's gone that bloody Richardson bloke get 'mself all drunk up and he shoot Jandamarra's young uncle in the back. Break 'm in the back. He can't move. He's dyin'. Richardson he leave 'm there on hill for dingo. He's laughin', that Richardson.

"But later Jandamarra come back with blackfella mob and he see his uncle there, layin' on the ground, all blood, all dyin'. When he saw it was his own uncle he cried, he wept. The uncle say, 'Richardson he's the one who done it. Shot me in the back. I can't walk no more, Jandamarra. I'm done. Finish me off!' Jandamarra didn't know what to do. But then he did it. He pull his revolver out quietly and walk behind and put a bullet in back of his uncle's head. 'I'm so sorry,' he told 'm. Oh, he was sorrowful. He cry and cry. He want to die himself. He don't want to go on livin'.

"He take that mob in chains back to Lillamooloora, back to p'lice station. He go to another blackfella tracker and tell 'm, 'I just kill my uncle. Now you finish me off, too. I just wanna die.' But that blackfella bloke wouldn't do it. So Jandamarra— Pigeon—he wait his chance to get back at that Richardson. All the blackfella mob there in chain by the tree they callin' out to Jandamarra, 'Oh, Jandamarra, you're nothin' but a white man dog,' they say. 'White man dog, that's what you are!' They tell 'm, 'Stop bein' white man dog, Jandamarra. Now you break our chain and let us go free! You come with us!'

"So Jandamarra he go to Richardson there at Lillamooloora and he tell 'm, 'I need rifle to go kill kangaroo for that blackfella mob over there. They hungry, they wanna eat, those jailbirds.' So Richardson he tell 'm, 'Oh you know where the gun is, mate. Over by the wall.' Then Jandamarra he go over by the wall, pick 'm up the gun, and come back to Richardson with it.

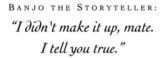

BANJO THE STORYTELLER:
*"I didn't make it up, mate.
I tell you true."*

Richardson ask 'm, 'Did you get the gun?' And Jandamarra say, 'Oh, yeah, I got it awright!' . . . and then Richardson turn around, and Jandamarra *he blow his head off!*

"Then Pigeon—Jandamarra—he go back to those blackfella jailbirds and he tell 'm, 'Awright now, you mob! Don't you call me "white man dog" no more. Now I'm gonna break your chain, gonna set you free, gonna get all of us outa here.' So he take the chain off his people, all of 'm. They go get guns and tucker from the p'lice station and then they run off back beyond into the hill. They kill 'm some more whitefella who try to catch 'm. They gonna take back their land, take back their country and be free again!"

BANJO PAUSED. His resonant, singsong tenor voice hung on the air. He was breathing heavily, obviously taxed by the telling of the story. He took several deep breaths, composing himself, then continued:

"P'lice they come after them blackfella. Gonna kill 'm all, that's what they gonna do. Plenty plenty p'lice, comin' all over. Pigeon and his mob they keep outa the way, hide 'mselves in Windjana Gorge, hide in hills. . . . P'lice they find 'm and shoot 'm, kill plenty blackfella, but Pigeon he get away from 'm. He's shot, he's bleedin', but he get away, hide out in Tunnel Creek. . . . They can't find 'm anymore. . . . Pigeon he's laughin' at 'm.

"So p'lice they bring more coppers up from Roebourne. Come to Derby in a ship, four funnel on it, big ship. Fifteen p'lice they was. They come to kill 'm. But they know they can't catch 'm, so they bring a blackfella tracker from Roebourne, blackfella named Mingo Mick. He's a witch doctor, you know? He's what we call a Maban, a magic man. He's the only one can catch Pigeon because Pigeon's a magic man too.

"Mingo Mick he follow Pigeon's track . . . up there near Tunnel Creek. Pigeon, he's shot again by the coppers, but still he gets away from 'm. Mingo Mick he come after 'm. Pigeon looks down from the mountain and he sees 'm comin' way down there. He knows it's Mingo Mick. He knows Mingo Mick's come there to kill 'm. He knows his time is come. So he fires a shot down at Mick just to let him know he's there.

"Mick sees 'm standin' way up there and comes up the mountain after 'm. When he gets to where Pigeon is, he finds Pigeon just layin' there, still bleedin'. Whitefellas say Mick shot Pigeon in the head, but that's a lie. Mick shot 'm in the thumb, cause that's where his power is . . . that's the only place he can die. His thumb. That's his power.

"So Mick shot Jandamarra and he cut off the thumb. He thinks he take Pigeon's power back on the ship to Roebourne with 'm, but Pigeon's spirit, it isn't dead, you know? When he knew he's goin' to die, he put his spirit in the water, down there at Tunnel Creek. Mingo Mick stopped to have a drink, and he could see Jandamarra down there in the water. Then he know Jandamarra's not dead. He know Jandamarra'll come get 'm, and he ran away, go back to Derby, get back on that four-funnel ship to Roebourne, tryin' to get away from Jandamarra's spirit.

"But he couldn't get away. Jandamarra's spirit came and blew up a big storm. Put a hole in that ship and sank it! Sank Mingo Mick and all them coppers. Sank 'm all! Drowned! They couldn't get away. Jandamarra's spirit see to that.

"Then Jandamarra's spirit come back to Tunnel Creek, back into the water. He's still there today. His face is lookin' up from the water. I go there many time and see 'm there. Maybe you won't see 'm, but he's there watchin' you. He won't talk to you Gadia blokes, but he talk to *us*. I talk to 'm many time. His spirit run around in that water.

"Jandamarra, he not bin dead, mate. Not forever!"

"THAT'S THE END o' the story," Banjo said. "I'm finish."

His heavy breathing subsided.

"So how did you go about learnin' that story, Banjo?" Mike asked him.

"Old men at night, they tell me that story. Bunaba people, my people. They tell us by the fire at night. I don't make it up, mate. I tell you true. It's my job to pass it on. Terence there, he know the story. And my little grandson Sammy, I teach it to him. When I pass on he be the keeper o' the story. Billy Oscar over in Fitzroy, he keep the story, too. He's number-two keeper. . . . Did he treat you blokes right?"

"Oh, yeah," Mike said. "He showed us around Tunnel Creek, told us some of the story. . . . Not as much as you, Banjo."

"I'm number-one keeper," Banjo said. "Whitefellas they come to me, tell me to tell 'm the Pigeon story, they wanna make movie, you know? I help 'm plenty time, tell 'm all the story, but still don't see no movie. Look here, I show you what them newspaper say. Gimme that bag."

He reached once more into the commodious interior of his dilly bag, his arm disappearing up to the elbow. I had the feeling he might plunge his arm into it up to the shoulder and then—huge as he was—fall into it altogether, as if that bag somehow contained the entryway to the Dreamtime itself.

"Oh, here," he said, pulling out a dog-eared scrapbook. "This'll tell you everything."

It was a souvenir album of fading press clippings and family-album-type photographs, many of them loose, thrown together in no seeming order. Among the clippings were some referring to a movie being planned on the Jandamarra story by a producer in Broome.

"It'd make a great movie," I said.

"Oh yeah," Banjo said. "I tell 'm whole story, and they say they gonna make it, that Jandamarra story."

"So when's it comin' out, Banjo?" Mike asked.

"Oh, I dunno. I dunno. Been a long time now. I don't hear from 'm much anymore. Mebbe Jandamarra he don't want 'm to make that movie. I dunno."

He looked at me, shrugging.

"You sure you puttin' that Jandamarra story in your book?" he asked.

"You bet, Banjo. Just the way you told it."

"That's good. People should hear it, that story. They should know Jandamarra was no bad man. Richardson was the bad one. Jandamarra he fought for his people, he die for his people. . . . People everywhere should know about him. You send me your book when you write it?"

"I will."

"Good. I wanna read it. You better tell it right, though, you hear? I'm gonna read that book and see if you told it right. Jandamarra . . . he be watchin'!"

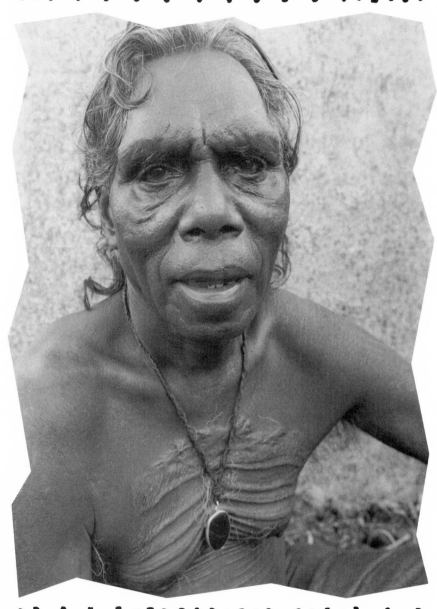

NGARINYIN ELDER DAVID MOWALJARLAI:

"I know who I am. I have my identity."

The Mystery of Wayrrull

"WHAT'S IMPORTANT IS beyond all understanding—that's the first thing you must understand," Ngarinyin elder David Mowaljarlai told us.

From the tortured topography of his remarkable face, his unfathomable eyes peered out at us as if from a great distance, at once fierce and gentle, projecting both power and pain. I tried looking directly into them but found my gaze overpowered by his. I had to look away for a moment, recompose myself, then lock onto his eyes again. Law Man's eyes. Dreamtime eyes. They had some terrible hurt in them.

"So I'll talk to you fellas awhile and speak of some things," he went on. "Ask me questions if you like . . . but remember the same question's got different answers for different people. Maybe they're true for you, maybe not. And never forget—*every-thing*'s a mystery anyway. Once it stops bein' a mystery it stops bein' true."

I knew immediately I'd come into the presence of an extraordinary mind and soul.

Law Man, philosopher, mystic, author—named Aboriginal of

the Year in 1991 for his lifelong efforts on behalf of his people —
David had recently returned from a spirit-journey of his own to
Scotland to retrieve seven crates of Aboriginal bones from the
University of Edinburgh, where they'd been kept for "research"
for more than a century.

"We must help these dead people finish their journey," he
said. "They were honorable people, they lived honorable lives,
they lived to teach their children. They deserve to be returned to
their land. If we return them to the land at a proper place, they
can return to the spirit world."

He was now about to leave for Sydney to give a series of lectures on Aboriginal culture and spiritual philosophy.

"I go teach in the universities in Perth or Sydney or wherever
young people'll listen to me. Give 'm one o' my messages. You
call 'm lectures, but they're messages. Words carry the spirit,
you know? That's about all we Aboriginals have left to give the
world. Spirit. But that's a lot, and we're always glad to share it.
So sit on down in the shade here. I'm glad you blokes caught me
before I left."

We sat on some plastic chairs beneath a shade tree in his well-
trimmed front yard. Back at the center of the Universe.

"*Identity,*" he began. "That's the thing."

WHO I AM

"I know who I am. I have my identity. I'm a Ngarinyin man. My
Dreaming is Hibiscus. That's my symbol, a beautiful pink
flower. And this . . . this also is my identity."

David pulled open the top of his shirt to reveal the most
impressive array of scars I had seen on any Law Man — a kind of
tapestry of pain inscribed across his entire upper chest and
torso.

His eyes burned with an incandescent pride.

"This is my brand, my identity. We have to spill our blood on the earth, spill our blood in the country to make it ours. Once we spill our blood there we belong to that country. When another Aboriginal looks at these scars, he knows where I'm from, what my country is, who I am. He knows my identity and I can look at him and know his.

"But these days my people don't belong to their country anymore. They been locked out. White man took the land away from them. Took their identity away, too. Our people don't know where they're from anymore. They don't know their grandfather or grandmother. They don't know why they're on this earth. They hurt. They hurt in their heart. They dry up like a desert. They're empty like an empty drum inside. Got no life inside 'm. That's why they want the grog so bad. To make the hurt go away. To make it wet again inside.

"So they get into all kinds of humbug and kill 'mselves and each other. People I knew who were young in the sixties and seventies . . . they're dead now. Gone. I have to bury 'm. But I'm an old man now . . . they should be buryin' *me!*

"And it's all because they don't know their right place. They don't know their country anymore. They don't know their borders, their boundaries. Everyone needs to know their place and where their border is. If they don't know that then they don't know their own identity. Without that they have no soul, nothin'. That's their creation place that country. When they die the soul goes back there. Doesn't matter where they die, their soul goes back to their country. But now their soul is lost. They never knew their country so their soul doesn't know how to get back there.

"Even worse, today's generation, they don't want to listen. They've lost it and they don't want to know it. They don't want to know who they are. So that's why I go around teachin' about

Aboriginal identity. Teach white people, teach black people. Teach 'm about Aboriginal culture. I'm tryin' to give the Aboriginal back his identity. . . . That's my work, that's my life."

THE LIVING BODY OF AUSTRALIA

David brought out a small drawing he'd made of "the body of Australia," depicting an approximation of the continental land-mass enmeshed in a cat's cradle of lines.

"This map is how things were a long time ago," he explained. "It shows the land the Creator gave us. This is Australia. We call it Bandaiyan. That's our name for it. See, this is where we are right here—Derby. And just above, that's my country in the Prince Regent area—Ngarinyin country. And down here, that's Perth and Geraldton on the west coast. Across on the other side, that's Grafton and Sydney on the east coast.

"It's all a body. A living body. See, it's got a head and neck, shoulders and ribs, pelvis and legs. The head—you can't really see it because it's up here, in the air. It's like we're looking down at the body. The Kimberley and York Peninsula, those are the lungs. Tasmania and the islands off the south coast, those are the feet. Down here in the middle of what you call the Bight of Australia, that's the pubic section. And right here in the center of the body is Uluru—you know Ayers Rock by Alice Springs—that's the navel."

"And what are those circles going around the outside?"

"Those show the outer limits—you know, like your 200-mile limit. That's as far as our border goes. Beyond there, past deep water, we don't own it. Those circular lines connect up the outer islands. All the Aboriginal island peoples who lived in those islands, they've almost all died out now.

"See all these spaces here between the lines of the grid block? . . . Those are the lands belonging to each people. We call it their Dambun. They're responsible for that piece of land.

The people of each family group in that Dambun must look after one special thing—a mountain, an animal, the grass, or perhaps a tree. That's their Ghee, their symbol. It's through our Ghee that we represent all the living creatures—the flying birds, the crawling creatures, the ones that live in the water, and so on. We represent each and every one of them through our Ghee. For me, as I told you, my Ghee is Bidderjurrad, the Hibiscus.

"So the Creator Wandjina gave us each the responsibility for a particular place—that place and no other. We're locked into that place. No other place can be home for us.

THE TRACKS OF THE WANDJINA

"Inside each Dambun, each grid block here, the land belongs to one people, one language. You can't go in there through the middle of that country without the permission of those people. To get from here to there when you leave your own country you've got to walk along these lines. Those are the only safe places to go. They're called story lines or song lines. The stories and songs tell you how to go along the lines. The lines are channels for exchanging goods. They're paths for messengers. They're tracks the Wandjina made for us to follow. And here, these little boxes where the lines come together, those are places where people come together, meeting places, places for ceremony, safe places.

"White man, when he came in here, he didn't understand about those lines. He didn't see the pattern they made. He trampled right over 'm. He still doesn't understand. He bulldozes the land for his mines and cuts through it to build his roads. That digs all that pattern out. Destroys it. You can't recognize it anymore. That land only exists now in our stories and in our songs and in our ceremonies. When the land dies, we die.

THE BODY OF AUSTRALIA

'CORPUS AUSTRALIS' —

BANDAIYAN

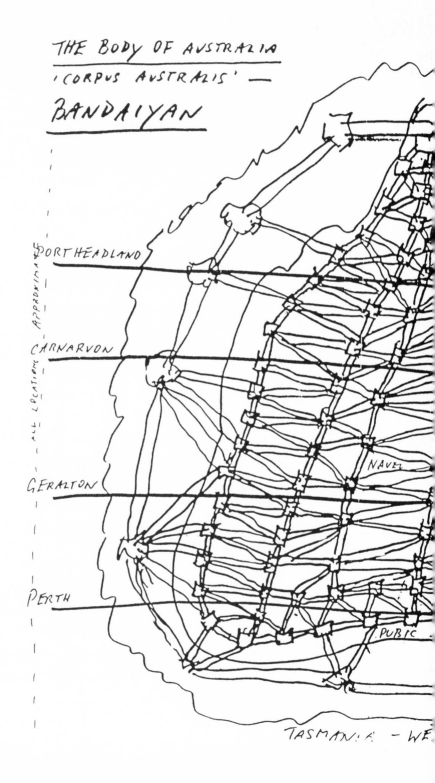

PORTHEADLAND

APPROXIMATE — ALL LOCATION

CARNARVON

GERALTON

PERTH

NAVEL

PUBIC

TASMANIA — WE

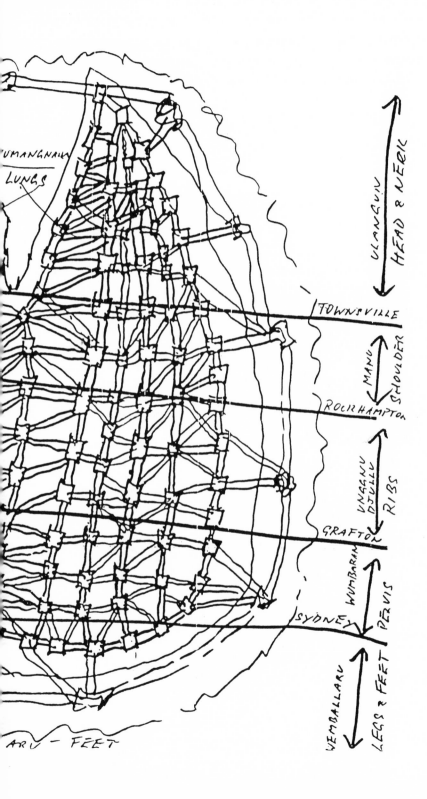

UMANGNAII
LUNGS

ULANGUN
HEAD & NECK

TOWNSVILLE

MANU
SHOULDER

ROCKHAMPTON

UNGANU
DJULU
RIBS

GRAFTON

WUMBARAN
PELVIS

SYDNEY

YEMBALLARU
LEGS & FEET

ARU — FEET

GOING WALKABOUT

"When I was a boy my father would take me around on walkabout all over this country. He taught me where the paths are, the safe paths to travel. He showed me where Snake walked in the Dreamtime, where Crocodile walked, where Goanna walked, where Dingo walked. We got permission from the other people to travel the land. We learned the songs and stories and had our ceremonies. We all went happily, learning how things happened in the long ago, in the Dreamtime.

"Now the people are gone from most those places. They don't come back. They don't repaint the Wandjina in the sacred caves anymore. The Wandjina waits for his children to visit him, but the children don't come back. Nobody's coming there to touch him up. The paintings get dull after the years go by. The Wandjina's sad and sorry to be left alone. Nowadays everything's sad, everything's sorry.

"So the only way we can remember him is with the stories. Whitefellas want to write 'm all down. But those stories are only supposed to be told back where we come from, back in our own country. The story really doesn't mean anything unless you can tell it at *that* place! They're not for reading in a book. They're for tellin' right *there* and nowhere else! They're for the people who own that country. They don't make sense anywhere else. They're not for someone's amusement.

"So that's why we need to be there, on our own land, in our own block, where we can repaint the pictures and tell the stories and contact the Wayrrull.

WAYRRULL — THE THRUST
BEHIND THINGS

"The Wayrrull—it can't be explained. It's a mystery. It's the power of the Wandjina. Wayrrull is the power that lets you speak. Wayrrull is the power of the motorcar. When a jet airplane roars and takes off, you hear the power of Wayrrull. Wayrrull is the thrust behind things.

"Wayrrull is in the grass, in the tree, in the river, in the mountain. . . . Wayrrull is in all Creation. Wayrrull, it's the power in everything. It doesn't matter where we walkabout, it's *there!* When we walk by a tree, that tree has this power—Wayrrull. We can see that tree because its Wayrrull, its power, contacts our eye. Wayrrull lets that tree talk to us. It tells us its story, that tree. The Wayrrull lets us hear. It speaks to us. Out of the Wayrrull we get understanding. We learn from it. It guides us.

"No, you *can't* understand it. No one can understand it. It's Wayrrull. It can't be explained. It's beyond understanding.

"That's how the Creator Wandjina made it for us. He made Wayrrull and he made it a mystery."

THE CREATOR WANDJINA

"Tell us about the Wandjina, David," I asked him. "When I talked to Daisy Utemorrah, she said there are many Wandjina and there's one Wandjina. I'm not sure I understand."

He smiled, nodding his head.

"Didn't I tell you it's beyond all understanding? Yes, there's many Wandjina and there's one Wandjina. That's true. Each Dambun, each of these grid blocks here on this map, has a particular Wandjina. The sum of all these Wandjina all over the grid is the Creator Wandjina."

"Is Wandjina the same as the white man's God?" I asked.

"Yeah, I suppose. God and Wandjina, they're the same. We all talk about one Creator. He created everything. In white man's lingo he calls him God. We call him Wandjina. But you can't explain Wandjina any more than you can explain God. Anthropologists say Wandjina was an Ancestor Being. To us Wandjina is Wandjina.

"Wandjina came from the wind and traveled the land and

made this earth, and the sea, and the mountains, the rivers, the water holes, the trees, the plants, the animals, the language, and the people. Wandjina made everything. Wandjina then gave us the Law to follow and gave us the land to keep forever.

"To Wandjina all our lands are just like a tiny speck, and so they see all things at all times no matter where we are on the land.

"All that they created is Ungud. That is to say, it is spiritual, possessing a powerful energy. Ungud is also Munma. That is to say, it is untouchable. Wandjina spiritual presence is in all living things. It's in the land itself. And it's in the universe, Ngadja, from where the Creator Wandjina looks over us."

REMEMBERING THE MYSTERY

David showed us a second line drawing—this one of a full-length Wandjina figure.

"I show this to the youngfellas so they'll know how to repaint the Wandjina someday. Somebody has to remember."

I knew from Mike that David had been involved a few years back in an attempt by the government to sponsor the repainting of some badly faded Wandjina figures at a sacred site in the west Kimberley. Despite his best intentions, his attempt had been the subject of bitter recriminations by traditional local elders, who claimed no one any longer possessed the right or knowledge to retouch the old paintings.

"David was stricken," Mike had told me. "He doesn't like to talk about it. He'd only wanted to save his culture from fading away and found himself under the most vitriolic attack by his own people. It broke his heart."

"Yes, somebody has to remember," David said now, showing us the Wandjina drawing he'd made. His fingertips stroked the flat white paper fondly.

"This is the Wandjina I've drawn here. The Creator Wandjina.

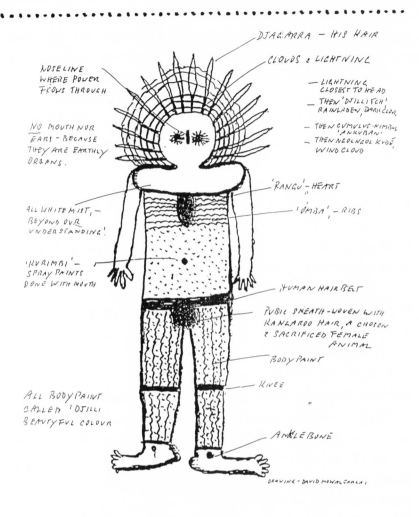

DRAWING - DAVID MOWALJARLAI

This shows all his different parts and how to paint them. The young people have forgotten all that. They never even knew. This'll help guide 'm someday when they go back to retouch the Wandjina, bring 'm back to life. . . . I just draw this picture with a pencil, you know, but it shows 'm where and how to put the paint. Maybe someday they'll want to do it. . . . Maybe someday they'll start carin' again.

"You see, look there around his head, that's his hair. It's made out of clouds and lightnin'. . . . He's all clouds, the Wandjina. White clouds. Black clouds. His body is mist. He brings the Wet season rains. He brings the wind. His voice is thunder, but he has no mouth or ears, see? Those are earthly organs, so he doesn't need 'm. It's all a mystery. . . . Everything's a mystery, never forget.

"See, here comes this dark cloud, that's his heart. It's dark and it's comin' low, comin' this way. . . . See it? You can feel the wind. You can see the lightnin' flashin'. You can hear him thunderin'. . . . He's comin' closer and closer. . . . Gettin' bigger and bigger. . . . He's a big black cloud coverin' the whole sky, glidin' across the whole world."

David's fingertips trembled on the paper. He was looking not at it but through it. That storm was out there in some different dimension, moving toward us out of the Dreamtime.

"We call him Gulingi," David went on. "He's the Creator Wandjina. He's sendin' us that storm. He's not there with the storm. We never see him. He's way, way back, sendin' it out to us. Sendin' his rain to us, sendin' the lightnin', sendin' his life to us. He put his picture on the walls to tell us who he is and who we are. He *is* that picture. We're his children, and we're supposed to repaint his picture, get back in touch with his Wayrrull. If we don't take care of the pictures, the rain won't come, the lightnin' won't come. Everywhere there will be destruction and death. The world will die and everyone in it. But nobody cares anymore. . . .

"He's our Creator. We've got to know and serve him. He gives us this earth. We're responsible for his Creation and everything in it. We're supposed to repaint him, but we're not there anymore. We're here in other people's country, not our own. That's why we hurt so bad. Because we're so far away from the Creator, so far away from Gulingi."

David's voice trailed off into a long, scratchy sigh. He grimaced. His pain was palpable.

"CAN THE AWTHA here put your words and drawings in his book, David?" Mike asked.

David nodded his head emphatically. "Yeah, I want you to do that. So people remember, you know? Remember the Creator. Remember the Wandjina. Remember Gulingi. That's my job, helpin' people remember. Help 'm remember the Mystery."

Markings

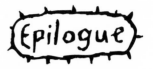

World's Edge

I WAS SITTING on a piece of driftwood at the edge of the world, watching a fireball sun stub itself out in the phosphorescent waters of the Timor Sea. A two-day drive along punishing outback tracks had brought us to this remote and spectacularly beautiful beach on the far northern coast of the Kimberley, where we'd parked the Land Ranger and made camp in a sandy clearing between four scrawny and arthritic-looking trees.

"Gubbinge trees they're called," Mike said. "There's a Dreamtime story a bloke once told me about this beach and these trees. Lemme toss some tucker in the pot and I'll tell it to you."

While he cooked up a savory steak-and-potato stew in an Aboriginal-style pit fire a few yards away, I returned to my reveries, letting my soul flow out and absorb itself in the *here* and *now* of that sunset. Streaks of electric orange and bloodshot red ignited the western sky. Out toward the horizon, a low island dissolved into lavender shadow. It was a fittingly otherworldly scene for this, the farthest edge of the "Land Beyond Goodbye" — about as far away from anywhere else as you can get on this planet without experiencing a primal gut fear of falling off.

Infinity, it seemed, lay just beyond.

I'D COME TO this far shore to get a sense of *beginnings*. . . .

Somewhere along this northern littoral, perhaps fifty to a hundred thousand years ago, perhaps more, the ancestors of today's Aboriginal people made their first entry into the isolated and unpeopled immensity of the Australian continent. Most likely they arrived during one of the periodic Ice Ages, when glaciers locked up much of the world's seawater and the oceans dropped several hundred feet below their present level. At such times small bands of wanderers could have made their way on foot down a swampy land bridge—geologists call it the Sahul—that lifted at times above the lowered sea, linking the continent of Australia to the great island of New Guinea just to the north. Others—among the world's first navigators—managed to island-hop in waterlogged rafts or rough log canoes from the Indonesian archipelago to this northern Kimberley coast, which extended a hundred miles or so farther out into the Timor Sea than at present. The nearest outlying Indonesian islands, submerged today, would then have been barely fifty miles from the Australian mainland, making it a difficult but still entirely feasible journey. With the melting of the Ice Age glaciers, inexorably rising seas would later cut off all contact with the lands of their origin.

Probably several, even many such migrations occurred over the millenniums, involving wholly different peoples. Nomadic hunter-gatherers, they had no agriculture, no architecture beyond bark huts and brush shelters, no pottery, no wheel, no metallurgy, no domesticated animals other than the dingo (a relative latecomer on the scene, arriving in Australia only about 6,000 years ago), and no weapons more advanced than spears, throwing sticks, and clubs.

Moving with the seasons, they wandered the bizarre landscape in search of giant kangaroos and other now-extinct megafauna, populating virtually the whole of the Australian continent by at least 20,000 B.C. Each small group existed in relative isolation from the others amidst the enormities of the continental interior. In an antipodean version of the Tower of Babel, they eventually developed several hundred languages and dialects. Staking out their own particular territories and commingling bloodlines according to strict and staggeringly complex rules of kinship, they gradually evolved an intricate web of cultural ties and social interrelationships, with similar ritual practices and spiritual beliefs revolving around the Dreamtime and Ancestor Beings such as the Rainbow Snake and the Wandjina.

SITTING HERE ON the beach at dusk, looking out across the fading waters of the Timor Sea, I conjured in my mind a vision of those first Australians scrambling ashore on this otherworldly Kimberley coast.

To my surprise — for I thought we were quite alone out here — an Aboriginal fisherman came walking toward me out of the sunset. He might have been walking right out of my thoughts.

Barefoot and spindly legged, with a barrel-bellied torso and an oversize head, he wore only a pair of ragged shorts. In one hand he carried a green plastic bait bucket sloshing water and in the other a large spool of filament fishing line. Over his shoulder dangled a passel of slim, silvery fish, each more than a foot long, still twitching as he walked, their long, spiky gills slowly opening and closing. He must have been fishing just the other side of a small peninsula of rocks not a hundred yards away.

I figured he was from an Aboriginal mission community we'd passed through an hour before on our way out.

He stopped and stared, contemplating the two of us and our Land Ranger among the gubbinge trees.

Surely he couldn't have expected to see a couple of white strangers in this unlikely place.

Was he the apparition or were we?

"Been fishin'?" I called out inanely.

No answer.

Emerging from the shadows into the flickering glow of our campfire, he seemed to flicker a bit himself. With his roundish face and short-clipped white hair and beard, he reminded me vaguely of an Aboriginal version of Popeye's father. A series of raised horizontal tribal scars pulled taut across his chest. It looked as if he'd once been tortured by the raking strokes of a razor-edged pendulum. Though obviously very old, they were so pinched and stretched they looked painful. And his feet . . . they were more like gnarled tree roots than feet, the black skin cracked like an old hide, the toenails horny growths askew at odd angles. They seemed prehistoric.

And yet, despite his ungainly shape, he was a magnificent human specimen, emanating a powerful physical presence and, with it, a tangy exudation of fresh seaweed, fish, and a strong animal musk detectable even over the smell of Mike's steak-and-potato stew. With the gills of the fish opening and closing over his shoulder, he looked in silhouette vaguely like a merman, as if he'd just risen from the sea.

I was about to offer him a cold can of soda pop from our Eski when he finally spoke, his gravelly voice friendly but firm. "Gotta go, mate," he said.

I assumed at first that he was referring to himself, but then he reiterated, "You blokes, you gotta go."

Mike looked up from his place beside the fire. "No worries, mate. Bossman over at the mission said it'd be all right for us to swag out here for the night."

The fisherman grimaced, twitching his broad nostrils and furling his shaggy white eyebrows.

"Not my bossman. Mebbe yours. He got no right, that fella. Not your place here. You better go like I say. Crocs round here, you know. Better you blokes sleep at the mission. Safer there. They got rooms."

"Those bloody rooms are worse'n closets," Mike said. "AC's either jiggered or too cold. We like it out here. Want a cold drink, mate? Got a full Eski here."

The Aboriginal man shook his head.

"Gotta go, you blokes," he insisted again. "Better go now, better get outa here. Take your bloody Toyota. You take me too. I can show you the way."

"I know the way," Mike said. "Glad to take you in the mornin' when we head back, though. Drop you off at the mission. By the way, tucker's cookin'. Care to join us?"

"No-o-o. . . . Gotta go. Bad place here."

He took a few tentative steps closer. I saw that his eyes seemed to have no whites around the pupils, only a tangled network of thick brown veins that picked up and reflected the firelight in a vaguely unnerving fashion.

"Gotta go, you blokes. Crocs'll be out tonight . . . you watch 'm."

"We'll chance it," Mike said, an edge of annoyance in his voice.

The man let out a disgusted snort and abruptly walked off, heading up the beach into some high reeds and within seconds dematerializing as if he'd never existed.

"Nice guy," I remarked to Mike.

"Some blokes'll say anything to cadge a ride," he said.

I remember reading that the first recorded words spoken by the Aboriginals to white settlers in 1788 had been *"Warra warra!"*—meaning, roughly, "Go away!"

That fit. Some things never change.

I recall also the first words spoken to me a decade before by a Ute medicine man on my arrival at his sheep camp in the remote desert wilds of southeast Colorado: *"When ya leavin'?"*

There had been no rancor in his voice, not even a hint of insult. He was simply making clear that, whoever I might be,

whatever I'd come for, I was less than welcome—in truth, quite
unwanted.

Although history, to my knowledge, doesn't record the first
words spoken by Native Americans to Christopher Columbus on
his arrival in the New World, I suspect they were along the same
lines.

NOW MIKE AMBLED over and sat down beside me on my driftwood perch.

"What's this he was saying about crocodiles?" I asked.

"No worry, mate. They won't come this far up the beach."

"How far *do* they come?"

"I said no worry. Forget it. Thinkin' only makes it so. You
wanna hear that Dreamtime story or not?"

"Sure. . . . I suppose. . . . Go on, let's have it."

"See that island out there, way out by the horizon? An old
Aboriginal bloke at the mission once told me about it. Mebbe he
shouldn't have, but he did. Seems that island was once part of the
mainland here, a peninsula, and a great serpent lived on it."

"The Rainbow Snake?"

"Mebbe, I don't know . . . probably a local version of it.
Anyway, the story goes, a cyclone came along one day and broke
the island off from the coast, takin' the bloody serpent with it.
The serpent, the story goes, couldn't swim. And since there
wasn't any water on the island and he needed fresh water to live,
he tunneled right under the ocean floor and came up here."

"Here?"

"Right where we're sittin'. Right here between these four gubbinge trees. You're sittin' on a sacred site, mate."

LATER THAT NIGHT, maddened by the unrelenting bloodlust of
the mosquitoes, I crawled out of my oven-hot swag and headed

barefoot along the nighttime beach for a meditative stroll. The tide was up and it was only a short walk now to the surf's edge, where the foaming, lukewarm waters of the Timor Sea lapped soothingly around my burning, sand fly–bitten ankles. By now the air had cooled a bit, and the sea breeze was a gentle caress on the skin. I breathed in the damp salt air, with its musky perfume of seaweed and long-dead fish. Somehow it was lovely, invigorating to the soul.

The thin clouds veiling the sky leaked just enough moonlight to cast a dim and ghostly luminescence over everything, giving vague shape to the contours of the beach, the gubbinge trees, and the rocky peninsula just beyond. The sea was a dark yet breathing presence out there, at once benign and monstrous. I'd come to the edge of the world . . . to the edge of the Dreamtime.

My stumbling spirit-journey into Aboriginal Australia was drawing to a close. I had originally envisioned it as a kind of "Journey into the Dreamtime," but it could never be that. At best I had skirted the edges of the Dreamtime. I could never get in. Nor should I. I'd gotten glimpses of it here and there, sensing it, divining it, almost sniffing it—but never crossing that invisible boundary and actually entering. I'd have to accept that. *"Get your own Dreamtime. Don't take ours!"* the Aboriginal man in the Hawaiian shirt in Wyndham had told me, and he'd been right. I'd have to keep working on that.

Digging my toes into the cooling damp sand, I focused on the *here* and *now* as best I could—remembering Reg Birch's words— but the present moment kept dissolving into memory. My mind ranged over the gallery of Dreamkeepers I'd met. Their memorable faces and words unreeled—unreel now as I write—before my inner gaze.

Certain key phrases haunt my mind:

David Mowaljarlai's "What's important is beyond all understanding. . . . Once it stops bein' a mystery it stops bein' true."

Banjo Woorunmarra's "Jandamarra, he not bin dead, mate. Not forever!"

Betty Johnston's "You gotta *buhLEEVE!* 'F you don't *buhLEEVE,* nothin' happen."

Reg Birch's "To change the world we have to change ourselves. . . . You must *become* the change you want to see in the world."

Ted Carlton's "We're all one family . . . we human beings. All one big mob!"

Daisy Utemorrah's "Just stop by and say hello to us, that's all we ask."

Well, at least I'd done that, Daisy. And for all my shortcomings, I'd found something infinitely precious here. I'll refrain from trying to define it or construct a philosophy around it in my Gadia way.

Let it remain a mystery, beyond all understanding.

I WONDERED WHERE that Aboriginal fisherman might have gone after his unsuccessful attempt to scare us off this sacred site with threats of crocodiles. Back to the Dreamtime? At least he knew where he belonged, even if he couldn't quite get there. Could I say as much?

Now an ominous scratching in the sand snapped me abruptly back into the *here* and *now*. I heard heavy breathing from somewhere behind me along the beach. I immediately dismissed any thoughts of crocodiles. After all, as Mike had often reiterated, "Thinkin' only makes it so." Maybe Mike himself had decided to follow me on down here? Or, perhaps, the Aboriginal fisherman?

But, no . . . turning around I saw an ugly-mugged black dog of medium size a few yards off. He was sitting on his haunches, lips aslobber, eyeing me with rapt expectancy. Likely a camp dog from the mission community. A good goanna dog like George

Wallaby's, no doubt. He'd probably smelled Mike's steak-and-potato stew and was hoping for a few scraps. I reached out tentatively to give him a friendly pat on the head, but a barely muffled growl and show of sharp teeth made me pull back my hand.

Oh, well. . . . I'd keep my distance if he'd keep his. As David Mowaljarlai had said, *Everyone should know their place and where their borders are*, right?

Righto, mate.